Cadbury's
Second Book of
Children's
Poetry

Beaver Books

A Beaver Book
Published by Arrow Books Limited
17–21 Conway Street, London W1P 6JD

An imprint of the Hutchinson Publishing Group

London Melbourne Sydney Auckland
Johannesburg and agencies throughout the world

First published 1984
© Cadbury Ltd 1984

Cadbury Limited and the Publishers have taken every possible precaution to ensure that the material in this book is the original work of the named writers and does not infringe the copyright of any person or body. Each poem has been authenticated by a responsible adult and the work has been carefully checked by independent experts for plagiarism. If despite this we have inadvertently failed to identify any borrowed poem we would be grateful if this could be brought to our attention for correction at the first opportunity.

Set in Linoterm Souvenir Light by
JH Graphics Limited, Reading

Printed and bound in Great Britain by
Cox & Wyman Limited, Reading

ISBN 0 09 937320 3

Contents

Publisher's note

The poems in this book were chosen by a panel of judges which included poets, teachers and educationalists, from nearly 20,000 entries for the Cadbury's National Exhibition of Children's Art 1984/5. This year is the second in which there has been a poetry section and the judges – Joan Freeman, educational psychologist; Jack Dalglish, Staff Inspector of English and poet; Vernon Scannell, poet; and Jennifer Curry, anthologist and author – were delighted at the great variety of material. They chose as outstanding the work of Lisa Robinson and David Woodhouse, whose poems appear on page 145 and on 54 and 168 respectively.

David Woodhouse is now sixteen and lives in Hull. He is studying for his O levels at present and hopes to read English or History at university. He is a clarinettist with the school band and is interested in cricket.

Lisa Robinson is now fourteen and lives at Clacton-on-Sea. She, too, is studying for her O levels. She has been playing the violin since she was eight and is also interested in ballet. Her poem, *Frog*, is about her own pet frog.

The judges also highly commended thirty-three children whose poems appear on pages 7, 8, 21, 22, 30, 34, 36, 38, 41, 48, 68, 69, 80, 83, 87, 90, 92, 118, 120, 126, 127, 132, 139, 140, 141, 144, 146, 148, 150, 166, 167, 170 and 188.

The poems have been arranged under subjects which gives the reader the opportunity to compare the ideas of children from as young as six to mature seventeen year olds. All the illustrations are taken from entries to the Art and Craft section of this year's Exhibition, and they complement the poems in an unusual and satisfying way.

We are very happy to be publishing such an interesting and original book and would like to thank all the writers and artists for their superb efforts. Don't forget, there's another chance to see your poem in print in the third *Cadbury's Book of Poetry* to be published in 1985. For details on how to enter next year's competition please turn to page 208.

Foreword by Sir Adrian Cadbury

Although the National Exhibition of Children's Art has made a significant contribution to Art and Craft education for 36 consecutive years the Poetry section is a very recent addition. We are, in fact, only at the beginning of the second year; but we introduce the *Second Book of Children's Poetry* with confidence born of the success of the first book and the ease with which poetry has taken its place in the context of the total Exhibition.

We have no doubt, from the sustained high level of entries from aspiring young poets and the interest displayed by the general public in the book, that poetry is now established as a continuing and important section. Cadbury Limited will again donate a Royalty from the sale of the book to the Save the Children Fund which is an obviously appropriate Charity.

All entries are painstakingly scrutinized by preliminary judges and by an Advisory Committee of leading poets and educationists. They have been impressed by the colour and spontaneity of the work of the younger children and by the imagination and originality of those at the top of the age range.

We believe that you will derive as much pleasure from reading the work of our young poets as we did from organising and judging it.

Adrian Cadbury

'My Self-Portrait', Akhvinder Mandhar (8)

Being Me

School

I can read and write
    and spell,
I can add up sums as well.
I can take away and
    multiply,
I can draw aeroplanes
    in the sky.
I can tell what is big
    and small,
I do PE and play football.
I can see what is red and
    blue
And pink and green and
    orange too.
I go swimming at the
    pool,
All this I have learnt at
    Harenc School.

Robert Hageman (6)
(Highly commended)

Just a Dream?

In Shrewsbury when I was four
I had a long green garden,
And every day when I looked out
A big white van was there.
But always now when I ask my Mum
About that long green garden,
'No,' she says. 'That garden was small,
And no big white van was there.'

David de Boer (11)
(Highly commended)

Where?

I'm sure this is right . . .
Well, almost . . .
It's now so confusing, I really don't know . . .
I've been here before . . .
I'm certain . . .
But now which way do I go?

This road looks familiar . . .
But no . . .
It's only a cruel trick of the light.
Things may be clearer
Ahead . . .
But now should I go left . . . or right?

I must have taken
A wrong turning . . .
It's getting dark; I can hardly see.
Mum and Dad
Must be worried sick
Waiting, waiting at home for me.

No one else
Is around . . .
I'm tired, hungry, and in despair . . .
I seem to have tried
Every possible route . . .
So where can I go now? Where!?!

Joan May (11)

Climbing

I sat upon the window-ledge,
Then struggled to the door,
I tried to climb the ceiling,
But fell upon the floor.

I climbed up to the mantelpiece
And tried to reach the key,
I slipped upon the flower pots,
And landed on my knee.
Determinedly, I clawed the wall,
And kicked out at the light,
My hands got stuck to paper,
I dangled there all night.

But now I'm old, and can't get down,
My legs I'm sure are dead,
Old hands and neck have got the cramp,
And getting down I dread!

Fiona Hunter (14)

'The Missing Sister', Dawn Michelle Crowther (16)
(Highly commended)

Staring at the Wall

I sit staring at the wall
In front of me.
Starting at the ground, it rises up
Skyscraperwise and windowless
Above me. Red bricks are growing in my mind.
In the wind the wall sways and leans:

It must not fall.

Kirsty Seymour-Ure (17)

Remember Me?

Remember me? I was your daughter,
The one you gave birth to
All those years ago.
Your hair was golden
And your eyes blue then,
Remember?

Remember me? I was your wife,
You used to drive me to the country
And we'd walk for miles . . .
And you'd take me on long weekends,
And cuddle me when I was cold.
Remember?

Remember me? I was your mother,
I used to powder you and change
        your nappy,
And rock you to sleep –
And love you
Yes, I used to love you
All those years ago.
Remember?

Remember me? I'm the senile patient
In ward 204.
The one who screams at night
        for some visitors.
But no one comes,
The one who mopes for her past –
Who throws food at the
        walls
And hits nurses.
Remember?

Jacqueline Kain (14)

I Scream

Chasm foreboding and foul,
I scream, my mouth wide as
      owls' eyes.

Echoes spectral form,
Across the chasm zoom.

A hand grotesque bursts from
      chasm dark.
And snaps at the echo,
      a venus fly trap.

The hand whirls.
The echo swirls round on
Imaginary string.

It returns, homing in,
A bat after prey.
Swoops back to the hand as
      if caught in a magnet.

Again it returns, fainter, more
      fragile,
Caught in the gravity of the
      hand.

It writhes to return again,
The hand pulls violently,
The echo collapses like a
      torrent of rain, into –

A chasm foreboding and foul,
I scream, my mouth wide as
     owls' eyes.

Gary Savage (12)

First Day at School

'I am not going!'
My mum grips my hand
Assuring that it's fun.
Suddenly!
Gates stare at me
That are bigger than my dad.
'Do they eat shredded wheat?'
They open
I walk in
Boys run about
Shouting.
A lady walks up.
'Whose mummy are you?' I say.
A bell rings,
Then a whistle blows.
Children walk in a big, big house,
Doors shut like prison gates.
My mummy's hand leaves mine
My last words are . . .
'Please look after teddy!'

Melanie Louise Skipper (11)

When I Sit Alone

When I sit.
I sit alone.
When I sit alone.
I sit by the fire.
When I sit alone by the fire
It warms and comforts me.
When I sit alone by the fire, warmed and comforted,
It keeps me company.

Douglas Moore (11)

Toes

I just *can't* get to sleep,
But I know what I'll play,
Every night it's the same
To my mother's dismay.

I'll pull back the bedclothes
And slide out my feet –
'Ten toes are now starring
in "Nutcracker Suite"!'

There's a mark on the big one,
It's been there a year,
Since 'what Aunt Maud did'
When she berthed in her chair!

The spotlights are on them
(This flexilamp's brill!)
I'll tear up some tissues
For skirts with a frill.

14

My nails are like birds' claws!
It's the latest 'in' look!
If you pull your toes up –
There's a stand for your book.

'Enter – Sugar Plum Fairy'
(Keep the rest in the wings –
tucked under the bedclothes.)
The telephone rings.

Mum creeps up the stairs
But the fun hasn't ended –
She played that in school
And was nearly suspended!

Nicola Jane Field (10)

A Thought

When we are hungry we eat sweets and
When the sweets are hungry they eat our teeth.

Mark Raven (8)

This Nose

I have had this nose for a long time
Longer than I can remember.
This was the nose that discovered Vick
This was the nose that my tongue tried to lick.
This was the nose that was painted bright red
This was the nose that helps me breathe in bed.
How funny people would look without noses –
How would we smell those beautiful roses?

Joanna Clare Desmond (10)

I Wonder

I wonder who thought of the alphabet,
And of telling the time.
I wonder who thought of the bad things
Murder, lies and crime.

I wonder who thought of the basin,
The bath or the kitchen sink.
I wonder who thought of the classroom,
Paper, pens and ink.

I wonder if I will ever know,
Why all the birds have wings.
I wonder if I will ever know
Any of these things.

Lesley Allison (11)

A List of Useful Things

A piece of string,
A safety pin,
A penknife, not too sharp.
A paper clip.
An orange pip,
A hook for catching carp.
An envelope,
A bar of soap,
A fly with plastic wings.
And now I have,
A list complete,
A list of useful things.

Sasa Jankovic (10)

If

If I were a shepherd
That the Angels came to see,
To tell me of a new birth,
That would mean the world to me.

Would I have taken my best lamb
That was perhaps a whole week's pay,
And given it to a baby,
That was born on Christmas Day?

Would I have really believed
What the Angels said was true,
That this little baby was God's only son,
I'm not sure I would, are you?

If I were a wise man
Would I have gone so far,
With nothing more to guide me,
But a shining star.

I've never seen an angel
Or such a shining star,
I've never ridden a camel,
Or travelled very far.

But I have read my Bible
And know the story's true,
That Jesus came from heaven,
For me and also you.

Janey Mitson (9)

Close Encounter in the Bathtub

I was sitting in the bathtub getting nice and clean,
When from underneath the water came a Russian
    submarine.
And then in his best English, the captain said, 'Ahoy!
Can you tell me how to get to Portsmouth Naval
    Base, young boy?'
He was tall, with a moustache, and on his left cheek
    was a scar,
I could tell that he was Russian for he wore a Soviet
    star.
I thought, 'Aha! now I see, he must be a Russian spy!
And so I didn't tell the truth, instead I told a lie.
The captain said, 'Now hurry up! Are vee on ze right
    courth?'
And I replied, 'Oh no you're not, 'cos Portsmouth's in
    the North!'
I tried to speak in Russian, 'You'll not bother me
    again!'
And then I pulled the plug out and he went straight
    down the drain.

Harrie Hayward (11)

What my Mum and Dad Think of Me

My mum thinks of me as a squirrel,
Because I hoard away lots of rubbish:
Plastic Bags
Old Clothes
Bits of string and cardboard.
My mum thinks it's unnecessary
For me to hoard away all this stuff.

My dad thinks of me as a silly human being
Because I spend all my pocket money on rubbers.
I do this because I collect them
I have about a hundred.
My dad thinks why do I need them,
He says I must need them because of all the mistakes
He thinks I make.

My brother thinks of me as an
Annoying pest.
He thinks this because when I play
A game like
Housies,
Secret Hideouts,
I always need something that
I don't have.

My hamster thinks of me as a
Kind-hearted girl.
He thinks I love him and care
For him, which I do.
He is the only one who loves me!

Tanya Berthond (9)

The Night

When I am tucked up in bed
the night hovers over me,
like a blackbird.
Then,
like an owl,
it swoops away
when the light comes.

Jane Hugo (9)

S-t-r-e-t-c-h-i-n-g

Waking up
in the morning
is lovely,
Especially when you s-t-r-e-t-c-h.
You open up
your legs and arms
and stretch.
It's just lovely.
The feeling just makes
you want to do it
over and over again.
But after a while
your stretch
runs out
and it's over.

Sharon Cheeks (10)

The Wind

I love to hear the wind,
Whistling through the trees.
When I go to bed,
I feel the lovely breeze.

I love to see the wind,
Picking up the leaves,
Making little roundabouts,
Underneath the trees.

I love to feel the wind,
Ruffling in my hair,
I cannot ever see it,
But I know that it is there.

Gillian Venables (7)
(Highly commended)

There is a Dragon inside Me

There is a dragon inside me,
Bewildered, puzzled and confused,
   Snoring all day.

There is a dragon inside me,
Fearless, brave and bold,
   Spitting fire.

There is a dragon inside me,
Miserable, wretched and depressed,
   Ashamed of showing himself.

There is a dragon inside me,
Clumsy, unwieldy and ungainly,
   Tripping himself up.

Catherine Mary Chambers (9)

My Mouth

A cave in the middle of a head.
With stalactites and stalagmites joining each other
    to make columns.
Great balls of fire enchant the back of the cave.
A hatchway to go down if cyclones come.
A fur rug laid down on the stone floor.
With snakes underneath wriggling in and out
In curious ways in a cave in the middle of the head.

Andrew Drought (7)
(Highly commended)

Honey for Tea

I like honey for my tea
Please busy bee give some to me.
I have my tea at five past five
I know you make it in your hive.

I like to spread it on my bread
And eat it before I go to bed.
To spread it on the bread is tricky
Because it is so very sticky.

James Forward (6)

Whispering

One day I was a-walking,
When I heard a rustling sound.
It sounded like the tall trees
Whispering to the ground.

I leaned against the tree trunk
And quietly heard it say,
'Watch out, watch out, the wind's about,
And he's very cross today.'

So I ran home to my mother,
And told her straight away,
'Watch out, watch out, the wind's about
And he's very cross today.'

Annabel Smith (7)

Cleaning Teeth

Teeth are very precious,
We need them all the time,
To eat our food and chatter
So I look after mine.
I brush them every morning,
I brush them every night,
I brush them up and down
To keep them sparkling white.

Lisa Welsh (6)

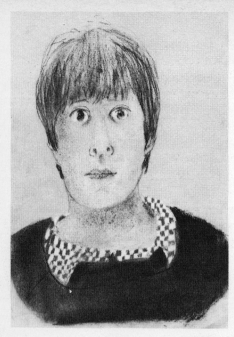

'Self Portrait',
Adam Gutteridge
(8)

Me

I have feet
Toes that meet
Eyes of brown
And a frown.
I can dance
Go to France
I ride a bike
And do what I
LIKE!

Jennifer Gresty (7)

24

My favourite food

I like cakes with pink icing.
I like chocolate with biscuits.
I like soup with toast in.
And I like to taste a piece of pastry.

I like crunchy apples.
I like crispy toast.
I like to nibble a piece of cheese,
I like fish and chips with peas.

I like Jelly on a plate,
I like to eat a grape.
I like sausages and chips,
I like cold chicken with gravy on it.

Kate Miller (6)

Eating Sweetcorn

Hot, dripping with butter,
A real treat.
You pick it up and it becomes wild.
Butter escapes.
It runs all over your hands,
Over the plate and your mouth.
You bite into an unknown world,
Of hills and valleys,
Each one waiting to be searched.
And when you have finished,
Your job is done.

Vanessa Hill (11)

'My Mummy', Kerri Truscott (3)

Other People

My mummy

My mummy is middle size.
Her shoes have holes in.
And sometimes she gets brown at the beach.
My mummy is podgy but funny.
My mummy is sexy and always wearing suspenders,
And she loves Chinese takeaways
Chocolate and my sweets.

Danielle G. Bemmer (8)

A Protest Poem on My Sister

Who went and told mum I'd
hidden her false teeth?
Who stole my last piece of
Edinburgh Rock?
Who borrowed my calculator and
hid it in the cupboard?
Who told Mrs Davies mum was 63
And blamed it on me?
Who gave me a pound,
And called me a thief?
My sister stares up in innocence,
And then in disrespect cries out,
'Well it certainly wasn't me!'

Ewan Moore (9)

Daddy

He was . . .
a boy who became
a man
a husband
a father.

He is . . .
a good tennis player
rotten at handstands
not bad at headstands.

He is . . .
a man who does jobs well
who enjoys his meals
never stops at the pub
and sneezes very loudly.

He is . . .
a man with a good temper
a man who jokes
and who is very clever with wood.

He is . . .
a very neat writer
often solves problems
and is very kind.

He is . . .
. . . my Dad.

Lisa Jenkins (10)

My Dad

My dad is blue
He is a windy Autumn day
My dad is a deep dark dungeon
He is a hurricane
My dad is a pair of dirty jeans
He is a filing cabinet
My dad is the nine o'clock news
He is a very hot curry.

Tariq Hussain (8)

'Daddy', Alison Kathryn Pursey (5)

Why? Why? Why?

Why is your nose so big, dad?
Why are there leaves on a tree?
Why is water wet, dad?
Why won't you listen to me?

Why is the grass always green, dad?
Why is the sky always blue?
Why do I go to school, dad?
Why do I always sneeze? Atshooo!

Why did you marry mum, dad?
Why is your hair turning grey?
Why do you boss me around, dad?
Why won't you let me play?

Why does a cat have four legs, dad?
Why are you blocking your ears?
Why do the clouds float around, dad?
How old will you be in nine years?
Why, dad? Tell
me why.

Emma Hulme (11)
(Highly commended)

Mealtimes

We love to eat at Nana's,
Because the food's so good.
There's lamb and ham and turkey
And beef with Yorkshire pud.
But better than the best of these
We like the cabaret,
Which Grandad always does for us,
And it makes Nana say
'Alec, peel the veg,
Don't let the custard burn.
Answer the door and where's my shoes,
Take off that shirt it's torn.
Peel the sprouts and where's my bag,
That gravy's much too thick.
Mop the floor, don't make a mess
and Alec do be quick.
Hoover the floor and feed the cat,
And make the strawberry flan.
There's just one thing I can't abide,
And that's a lazy man.'
And when at last poor Grandad comes,
To sit down at the table.
Nana gets him up again
As fast as she is able.
To make herself a cup of tea,
That's hotter than the last.
And woe betide you, Grandad,
If she doesn't get if fast!

Janey Mitson (9)

Baby Breakfast

Squidge
My food in my fist
Throw
It at the wall
Rub
It in my hair
Soak
It in my milk
Squeeze
The dirt out
Stuff
It in my mouth
Splurt
It across the room
Dig
It out of my bib
Catapult
It to Mummy
Aim
It at Daddy
Mmmm
Finished.

Julia Marsden (15)

The New Baby

Three days left.
Mammy can't wait.
I can't wait.
The baby's due.

I wonder what
It will be?
Could it be a boy?
I hope so.
Mum does too.
Last time, the baby died.
Wee Paul.
We buried him up the hill
On a summer's day.
I was sad
I cried and cried.
Mum did too.
But now we're glad.
Three days left.
Uncle bought the pram,
Dad got the cot.
Louise knit a scarf.
I'm waiting for a brother.

Sara Brennan (9)

New and Special

Special,
Some things are not.
New things can be special,
Like Timothy's soldier.
On his birthday his mother bought it.
Its uniform was black, red and white.
Every day he played with it,
Knocking it down,
Shooting at it
With his cork gun.

But when it got old,
The paint began to peel
And its colours began to fade.
But his mother came in from shopping,
'Shut your eyes and stretch out your hands.'
'A brand new soldier,' said Tim.
Every day he plays with it.
'And that's something special,' said Tim.

Justin Cook (10)

January's Child

Too late for summer birth;
Too late even for autumn awakening,
The January Child
Lived out his first days in the cold
And the grey,
With snow on the ground
And frost in the air;
Little wonder that his face was pinched
And his fingers clenched and blue.

Too black and white and grey to survive in the
    coloured summer,
Too austere for pastel springs
And friendly shades;
The January Child
Must hate us so for knowing him
Yet still more bitter is he
When we pass him by.
Little wonder that the child lives as frost
Yet still seeks the warming summer people.

Too innocent and new for earthy passions deep,
Too worldly-wise and old for child-like innocence,
The January Child
Boils inside like molten rock
Yet never melts his ice,
Nor can he quench his thirst.
He weathers like the stone.
Little wonder that he cries
As all the world squeezes blood, and their pound of
    flesh, from him.

Too stubborn for any compromise,
Too yielding to stand as firm support,
He finds no friendship offered
By those who have no sympathy with his
'Other side'.
Watch him grow, twisted yet fine,
Stunted yet strong.
Little wonder that he needs his sharpened shaft
To pierce even those he seems to love, right through
    to the heart.

Too late for softly tinted summer ending,
Too late even for the crackling autumn's dying sigh,
The January Child
Dies, as he lived; in a strange land;
And in strange arms.
Dies in the grey dawning of a new youth,
And the grey twilight of a passing age.
Little wonder that in the birth of spring
We let our own darknesses lie forgotten.

Rachel Naylor (15)
(Highly commended)

For Annie

Night falls
Stone breathes into air
Slipping out into night.
The well of Deep Wind
changes into a mist of
feathers.
The mist changes into nothingness.
The silent steps shake the broken air
and whispers fall into
a sleep of silence.

Sean Borodale (10)

A Boy called Mad

The boy screamed through the laughing forest
Eyes alight with sunburnt glare,
Unseen voices ripped his senses,
Aural claws scathed his sight.
Sharpened sunlight slashed his sanity
Scarring his clothes with blurred memories,
As the laughter ran its fingers
Through the boy's fear,
And frightened lightning scattered his stride.

In the cell
Silent thunder numbed his mind.
Shades of bladed darkness
Bathed his tortured mind.
Mourning and shadows
Veiled his tears,
Sorrow from another boy
Pleading to return.
Staring through sightless eyes
His tunnel became darker.

The boy laughed through the weeping desert,
Icicle warmth clasped his legs
Tired of the run.
He felt
Broken light, sickening heat,
Sanity's hunger piercing deep.
The boy felt fear's velvet blow
Sampled its deadening drug.
Cacooned in a chaotic paradise,
Bled by
That sharpened blade of nonsense,
That cancer of the mind,
Insanity.

Marcus Collings (16)
(Highly commended)

Crippled Child

Why can't I get up, Mum?
The sun is streaming past the trees,
Into my bedroom lair,
And now and then I catch the breeze,
Soft and salt with the morning air,
And the curtains faintly whisper
Of how the wind doth blow,
And where the birds are singing most
Alas, they whisper low.
I strain to catch the sounds of life
That flutter from our road,
They float away from hearing
Elusive, unbestowed.
And the clatter of the children's play
That's drummed into my ears,
Leaves me sad with hazy memories
Of those carefree distant years.
Oh why can't I get up, Mum?
And be just another child.
With that child's unchosen future,
Running free and running wild.
The sun is streaming past the trees
Into my bedroom lair,
And sometimes when I catch the breeze,
Reality takes flight,
And I'm walking on the windy shore,
The only soul in sight.
With the shingle rattling in my shoes
Fine droplets in my hair,
And I'm talking with the raging sea
Which jeers at all my cares.
Or I'm cycling down a gusty hill
Or walking in the rain,

Or wending through the woods until
My dreams dissolve again.
And I'm left to live with feeble hopes,
And withered stalks for legs,
That fell upon the slopes of life,
Before the race began.
Why can't I get up, Mum?
No, don't tell me why, just leave,
And if you hear frustrated sobs
Just smile and say 'It's teens'
For I'll not live as you have lived.
So leave me to my dreams.

Emma Crates (13)
(Highly commended)

'Old Coates Mill, Paisley',
William McKenna (14)

Who's the Hero?

You were the big boy,
Always played it cool.
The hero's now a soldier,
Or is he just a fool?

You're the hero
If you fight.
You're the hero,
Sign tonight.

Vict'ry cries in your head,
You left to win the war,
Nobody ever told you,
But now you know the score.

You're the hero
If you fight.
You're the hero,
Sign tonight.

All your mates lie dead,
You say you never knew.
They pin medals on your shirt,
Who's the hero, is it you?

You're the hero
If you fight.
You're the hero,
Sign tonight.

Alan Stevens (14)

Yesterday's Hero

In other people's cast-off clothes
And worn out shoes on worn out feet,
See the lonely vagabond wandering
Through his winter years;
A fading shade of the man that was.

And did he ride the midnight sky,
Planing down the star-bright heights,
A golden God on silver wings,
Or avenging angel, disciple of Thor?

Was it thus;
And was it so?

From out his grey November face
His eyes, more vague than morning mist,
Look out on scenes we cannot see
Where friend and foe, who both were
Men, went seeking immortality.

And did he battle in summer skies
Where young men fought in modern joust,
With losers plunged in fiery flight,
No Phoenix rising from those flames?

Was it thus;
And was it so?

Earthbound now, tired limbs are shackled
By the burdening chains of age,
But wandering mind still roams the past
Lost in the mists of time:
A hero of those yesterdays.

And did he fly the moonlit paths
On flimsy wings and hasty prayer,
One of those they called The Few?
He still remembers. But do you?

For thus it was;
And it was so.

Joanna Crittell (14)
(Highly commended)

'Print of Figure', Simon Parry (14)

Margaret Thatcher

At number 10 Downing Street
There she sits,
Crossing jobs off the list.
Firemen's jobs,
GONE.
Policeman's job,
GONE.
Laughing away until the day
She gets put on the dole.

Vicky Harrington (10)

The Death of King Arthur

The night was cold, the wind was chill.
The mist swirled around and round.
The owls hooted as they flew from branch to branch.
The river was still and quiet.
King Arthur lay there,
A cold wound in his side.
The willow trees drooped as if about to cry.
The armour on his body glittered in the moonlight
    like stars on a frosty night.
Swiftly out of the shadows a boat floated silently to
    shore,
The tears of the three women aboard crystallized
As they hit the water.
The silence was deafening as he struggled into the
    boat to be taken far away until his services are
    needed again.

Alison McKie (10)

Momentary

Pale pink smile twitches to a halt,
Top lip sits tight and ominously on the protruding
    bottom one,
Tiny countenance angers,
Wrath feeds colour to its face
turning it into a quivering strawberry.
Eyes, damp blue, peer over mounds of compressed
    cheek,
Send forth hot tears that slide down the contorting
    nose
and are caught by a fat exploring tongue
Then whipped and concealed in its mouth,
The salty taste is examined.
    Suddenly, two pale eyes rise in wonder
over the subsiding cheeks.
A rich secure chuckle rises from his toes
causing the tight creased nose to unfold.
Red anger drains away like flood water.
The little body relaxes
And it sinks to sleep,
In a secure mass of white crocheted blanket
Like a little crumpled peach skin.

Lisa Robinson (13)
(Award winner)

The Postman

This is the postman making his journey,
Bringing the cards and presents all early.
Parcels for the rich, letters for the poor,
The bills and cheques all come through the door,
Walking through deep snow, a steady trudge,
The weather's against him, and the van won't budge.

Stuart Little (14)

The Vikings

They came unexpectedly
Creeping over the countryside
Like a huge cloud of death,
Their swords blinked and shone
In the darkness;
Eyes full of terror moved quickly through the night
As the reality of their coming took hold of them,
They paused and waited
And waited.
Then they attacked as surely as a panther
Sweeping towards its prey . . .

John Goulding (11)

The Hunter

Stealthily moving,
the hunter creeps through the forest.
Not a twig snaps at his feet,
No leaf is crushed by his weight.
Eyes pinned to the tracks of a deer,
Ears ready to pick up
the slightest sound.
Then! there-it-is . . .
A stag standing proudly by the river,
Coat gleaming brightly in the sun,
Antlers stretching out like the branches
of a young sapling.

A tingling sensation travels
down the hunter's spine.
Thoughts flash through his mind –
Should he kill this magnificent beast?
Should he leave it to live?
Its fate lies in his hands.
Slowly he kneels behind a thicket.
Beads of sweat run down his brow.
Silently, the rifle comes up to aim,
Heart pounding, the trigger finger tightens
its grip . . .
Then it happens!
The gun comes to life and
Fires!
As the bullet finds its target
The animal shudders and turns his head.
Large eyes look sorrowfully at the slayer
standing trembling before him,
Then, its great bulky body crashes like a felled tree
to the ground.
The hunter too collapses
Exhausted and, strangely, full of remorse.

John A. Burgoyne (10)

The Beachcomber

Between his toes the wet sands cling,
A chill wind tosses wild his hair.
The foaming seas their treasures spew
For him, a harvest of the waves.

46

'On the Beach', Richard Juby (11)

A lonesome jewel amongst the rocks –
The gleaming eye of a long-drowned God?
Or a sea-smoothed gem of cool, green glass?
Raw hands lovingly caress.

Distorted boughs of sea-carved wood,
Waterlogged, with sand ingrained;
Dredged up from some Armada's grave,
Or just a plank from the broken pier?

Tangled mass of cord and weed
Half-embedded in the sand;
Sea-horse harness from Neptune's steeds,
Or nets torn from a trawling ship?

The sea's strange gifts he gathers in,
Accepts them as a sacrifice
Like a God of days gone by;
The sea and man in harmony.

Joanna Crittell (14)

47

On a Fisherman

(My epigraph about a particular profession.)

A soul of swimming dreams,
In a storm of floods.
A varied life, of calm and rough seas,
In a haul of years.
Now, departed from life,
Gone from the nets of worry and despair.
Sailing in a boat to Heaven,
In a cargo of trust.
Buried with a seagull by his side,
The Fisherman lies.

Dawn Mann'a (13)

Mirror Mirror on the Wall . . .

First my lady stops to stare,
She twines a finger in her hair,
Then pouts and winks and smiles at me
And leaves the room quite happily.

Next the butler comes to gawk,
His thin fiddle face as white as chalk
Changes expression frequently,
He also leaves quite happily.

Now the master who strikes a pose,
Eager to show me his Roman nose,
He gazes at me contentedly,
He too departs quite happily.

I no longer think of myself as plain,
And I try so hard not to be vain,
But it is difficult, as you can see,
For everyone admires me.

Susan Szekely (16)
(Highly commended)

Cindy the Second

Cindy was a lousy brat,
She wanted this, she wanted that,
The ugly sisters went to town.
Left her sweeping up (and down).

Esmerelda was really chunky,
Ermintrude was awfully punky.
Buttons (the page boy) was pretty spiffing,
The rats in the cellar were always sniffing.

Esmerelda was awfully vain,
Ermintrude was just the same.
As for Cindy I don't know,
She couldn't care (what a blow).

Esmerelda and Ermintrude,
Came back from their walk in a very good mood.
They said, 'We're going to the Ball.
And Cindy isn't coming at all.'

Cindy watched them go to the palace,
She had to admit it, she was jealous.
Poor Cindy was locked up in her room,
She sat there in a heap of gloom.

The magic fairy came in sight,
Floating in a beam of light.
Cindy cried, 'Get me to the Ball,
The Prince is handsome (and very tall).'

Cindy's heart leapt awfully high,
She jumped, and almost reached the sky.
She bought a carriage, found a mule,
Put on a dress; and she looked cool.

Cindy always danced with a prince,
She squeezed him to a pound of mince.
What was the time? She heard a gong,
She thought, 'I'd better run along.'

Cindy ran out feeling bare,
She left her slipper on the stair.
The Prince ran out and grabbed the shoe,
And said, 'Ere's one. There should be two!'

Cindy ran home as fast as she could,
'Cause she had to make some Christmas Pud.
One sister yelled, 'The Prince likes you,
You stuck to him like a pot of glue.'

Next day the Prince came with the shoe,
But Cindy was in bed with flu.
The sisters tried to get it on,
And in the end the shoe was gone.

That is the end of this sad tale,
But I'm afraid it's not for sale.
Actually it turned out fine,
(The Prince asked Cindy out to dine).

Sarah Harkness (11)

50

The Gypsies

They know the hills,
They know the woods,
They know the roads,
And they know the country.

Scarlet hankies around their necks,
Ragged shawls upon their shoulders,
Threadbare jerseys, stretched and torn,
Colourful, flowing skirts.

They sit around the spitting fire,
And toast their tainted meat,
Aged women tawny with smoke,
Clothed in shades of brown.

Eliza Taylor (11)

The Old Man

The old man is an old oak tree,
Gnarled, bent, feeble.
His boughs creaking,
    Ready to break,
    Ready for death.
    Just waiting.

The old man is an old oak tree,
His trunk weathered and brown,
His skin rough, wrinkled, bark,
    Ready to flake,
    Ready for death.
    Just waiting.

The old man is an old oak tree,
Not scared but standing noble,
He has seen the whole world's history.
   Ready to wake,
   Ready for death.
   Just waiting.

Victoria Walker (14)

Sleeping Man

Old man sleeping
on the sand,
snoring
softly,
cap in hand.

Old tweed jacket,
holes are patched,
snoring
softly,
cap to match.

Glasses propped
upon his nose,
snoring
softly.
Dreams? Who knows.

Hands are clasped
across his chest,
snoring
softly,
he knows best.

Sleeping out there,
on the sand,
snoring
softly,
cap in hand.

Amanda Benmore (14)

The Madman

Not speaking, not talking,
Not seeming to hear,
He rocks quietly, slowly,
Backwards and forwards on
His chair.
Neglected by society,
He never used to be different.
Trussed up like a dog,
With his arms behind
His back,
He sits in his cell,
His padded cell,
Cocooned by anguish.
His face is expressionless,
Like a corpse,
But there is memory in
His eyes,
A memory which is fading.

Felice Pritchard (14)

Rugby League: As Expected

Nocker Norton,
Balding albino tiger,
The Boulevard mud
Does not lust for your body
As expected.

The inevitable massive tackle
Does not spread its muddy, muscled grasp
Around another passive Titan
As expected.

The humpty dumpty ball
Does not, when in your arms,
Smell another odious armpit
As expected.

But instead flashes like
A laser beam from
Your tinkling fingertips.
The crowd
Loves you
As expected.

David Woodhouse (14)
(Award winner)

Funny Sports

Daniel was a worried lad,
Asked Clare 'What's wrong with you?'
'Next is the three legged race,
And I have only two!'

'Marathon Runner', Lee Horseley (12)

Peter was the pole-vault king,
You've never seen the likes,
He didn't need to use a pole,
He sat on Steven's spikes.

Andrew won the slow cycling,
He said 'It was just luck,
I cycled through a patch of mud,
And both my wheels got stuck.'

Fatty won the tug of war,
The cup he proudly lifted.
The seven dumplings in his tum,
Made sure he wasn't shifted.

Ian Jones (10)

Boys Are ...

Something to lie awake about thinking of,
        Boys are.
  Something to admire,
    To watch from afar,
        Boys are.
  Something to sing about,
    To get nervous about,
To bite nails out about,
        Boys are.
  Something to feel sorry for,
    To adore,
Or simply feel are a bore,
        Boys are.
Something to write home about,
    To let your heart ring out,
  To murmur 'Yuk' about,
        Boys are.
        Dynamite,
        Delectable,
        Different,
        Maybe dull,
        Wide range,
        Wonderful,
        Worth it?,
        Boys ...

Marie Neeson (14)

Sea Visitors

A dull, grey mist hung over the sea,
As the white-topped waves crashed down on the
    shore.
A flock of gulls flew over my head,
And when all was silent, I thought I saw . . .

The dim grey figures of two small children,
In ragged dress of time long ago
Gathering sticks along the strandline.
I shouted to them, but they did not know.

I rubbed my eyes as two more figures
In grander clothes walked towards the sea.
I followed behind, but when they turned round
I'm sure that they could not see me.

But then they seemed to fade away,
And the ragged children had disappeared.
And I wondered, had they really been there?
Or were they just a dream, as I had feared?

Sarah Wallis (11)

A Witch's Spell

Into the pot goes a bottle of wine,
Into the pot goes a needle of pine.
Hubble Bubble,
Things to make trouble,
Into the pot they go.
Into the pot goes a jar of toads blood,
Into the pot goes a spoon of dry mud.
Hubble Bubble,
Things to make trouble,
Into the pot they go.
Into the pot goes a slice of dead frog,
Into the pot goes a chip of dry log.
Hubble Bubble,
Things to make trouble,
Into the pot they go.
Into the pot goes a big rat's head,
Into the pot goes a bone of the dead.
Hubble Bubble,
Things to make trouble,
Into the pot they go.
Into the pot goes a black cat's tail,
Into the pot goes a fin of a whale.
Hubble Bubble,
Things to make trouble,
Into the pot they go.
Into the pot goes a toad's wart.
Into the pot goes a bag of deadly malt.

Hubble Bubble,
Things to make trouble,
Into the pot they go.
Into the pot goes a wombat's knee,
Into the pot goes a bumble bee.
Hubble Bubble,
Things to make trouble,
Into the pot they go.
Into the pot goes a newt's egg,
Into the pot goes a mouse's leg.
Hubble Bubble,
Things to make trouble,
Into the pot they go.
Into the pot goes a dragonfly,
Into the pot goes a person's eye.
Hubble Bubble,
Things to make trouble,
Into the pot they go.
And after some stirring
And barking and purring,
And lots of loud whirring
We're left with a spell
For people who dwell, on the goodie-goodie world
To be withered and curled by the morning.
Hubble Bubble,
Things to make trouble,
Into the pot they go.

Marina Lavorgna (9)

When the Martians Came to Tea

They came down in cups,
(They'd not heard of saucers),
No flashing lights or noises,
But riding Martian horses.

They looked like mouldy beans,
All knobbly, but square,
With things round and pointed,
That maybe shouldn't be there.

They knocked upon the door,
And trampled in the yard,
They ate the hens and chickens,
But the dog was far too hard!

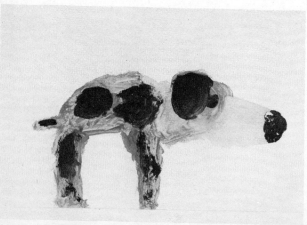

'My Dog', Phillip Barlow (7)

The lambs and sheep all disappeared,
Upon that very night.
The cat will never be the same,
She nearly died of fright.

They slid down the chimney,
And fell into the hearth,
They toppled down the toilet,
And gambolled in the bath.

They blocked up the drainpipes,
Slithered in the sink,
They ate the children's pen-sets,
And wallowed in the ink.

The furniture, it soon was gone,
The carpets and the 'phone,
They started on the brickwork,
And swallowed up our home!

Then as the break of day appeared,
The Martians said, 'So long!'
The cup zoomed back off into space,
I'm very glad they've gone!

Fiona Hunter (14)

'Kitchen Scene', Lisa Gordon (13)

The World Around Us

Sounds

The sounds in the evening
Go all through the house,
The squeaking and scratching
Of a little mouse,
The clanking of dishes
As dinner goes in,
The opening and shutting
Of the kitchen bin,
The ticking and tocking
Of the Grandfather clock
As it goes tick tock, tick tock,
The zooming of cars
Outside in the street,
The barking of dogs
At their owners' feet.

The hoot of an owl
Up in a tree
As it looks for its food
For tomorrow's tea.
The screeching of cats
Out in the road.
The zooming of lorries
Carrying a heavy load.

Joanne George (7)

Home

Solid heat,
Laboured movement.
Bustling in discomfort.
Oriental oddities in air-conditioned relief.
Wily shopkeeper, following tourists sly-eyed,
Expert con-artist gauging from one all-inclusive
    glance
How far he can up the prices; a good bargain they
    say.
Standing at his shop-door awaiting his unwitting
    prey,
Arms folded casually, inviting, enticing.
Smiling, but not smiling
With his inscrutable
Face.

Faces
Identical
Beautiful and seeming
Void of emotion as they plough home
Along choked alleys, piled high with rubbish,
To squalid, crowded boxes upon boxes, replete with
    family
And noise, and cooking smells from steamy kitchens.
Schoolchildren fight feebly with school assignments
While baby cries in Grandma's arms.
But they fight on, because
Work is success
And money.

Money,
The desired.
The answer to every question.
The one and only irrevocable status-symbol.
Procurer of great golden cars and elaborate funerals.
Foundation of dynasties: yet money is what brought
    me here,
To this place of concrete that is built from money,
That could not exist without it; and I find myself
Wanting, but never able to forget,
Somehow, the taste of spice,
The indefinable bonds
Of Hong Kong.

Joanne Hartley (15)

The Old School

Crumbling bricks in the wall of education,
Air vibrating with fractions and
        square roots,
Our school carries on,
Sentencing itself to eternity.

Rajeev R. S. Raizada (10)

'The Tree Outside the Art Room'. Paul Meadows (12)

This 'Ere School

This 'ere school is filthy,
This 'ere school is cold,
This 'ere school is full of rules –
Made for five year olds.

These 'ere teachers are boring,
I wonder if they're able –
To write non-stop an essay
Or to say by heart a fable?

This 'ere school's got children
Laughing by a wall
Maybe this 'ere school
Ain't so bad after all.

Stephanie Marshall (14)

Happenings – When the Clock Stopped

Monkey's grip drops
From the cage.
Tired housewife flops,
A busy day.
The vase is knocked,
But caught in time.
Teacher's preaching stops,
To catch his breath.
The fellow drops
His books in confusion.
Girl's eyes pop open
As the scales show '10st. 4'.
The blind man knocks
His foot on the lamppost.
The terrorist's shot
Another person
And the happenings happened,
  One day,
    One split second,
      In everyone's life,
When the clock stopped short . . .

Marie Neeson (14)

Hygiene

In the rumpled but clean
gleaming-white, uniform-sized
sleek, flat hospital bed
lay the old, fat, crumpled-up man
bound in by tight sheets,
smoothed down, plumped up
poked, prodded, examined
tutted over, blanket-bathed
tired by enforced rest and nurses' chatter.
At his side were marigolds,
chrysanthemums, roses,
all dead and dusty
in filthy smelly water.
They wanted to take them away
throw them away
but he would not let them,
his last rebellion against hygiene,
he had always wanted to rot away
in squalor and dirt, fall to dust
not pop off in a sterile bed
and be tidied away with the dead flowers.

Emma Payne (15)
(Highly commended)

Bedsitter Ballad

In the darkness I recall,
Remembering that last evening;
Throwing the lamp at the wall,
You left with no real meaning.

The bulb stays in fragments,
Never replaced;
As I lie in the darkness
Remembering your face.

Our love needed more
Than loose change in a pocket.
The gas fire starts to roar,
The metre costs a packet.

The bulb stays in fragments,
Never replaced;
As I lie in the darkness
Remembering your face.

We gazed at the ceiling;
Cracks turned to stars.
But you threw back the blanket
And left me in tears.

The blanket lying bundled,
Never replaced;
As I lie in the darkness
Remembering your face.

We sprawled on the mattress,
Drank wine from the toothmug,
Didn't care when we spilt it
Leaving stains on the rug.

It's still mottled and crumpled,
Never replaced;
As I lie in the darkness
Remembering your face.

Cracked sink in the corner,
The place where, in the morning
Performing daily rituals,
We sang to ourselves.

My hairs round the plug,
Lipstick on the mirror,
Your razor by the soap
Flung down with broken blade.

It's you I always think of,
Never replaced;
As I lie in the darkness
Remembering your face.

Lara Burns (15)
(Highly commended)

The Oldest Profession

Alone,
A girl,
Standing on the corner,
I look down
From my window
See her,
Standing there.
Jezebel.

Her object
The money
For services
Rendered
To make it
Worthwhile
She takes the cash first.
Jezebel.

Abandoned,
Mistrusted,
Providing a service,
Relieving,
Relaxing,
In dark
Midnight hours,
Jezebel.

Masking
The wrinkles,
The tell-tale lines,
Cosmetic
Beauty
To be seen
In the dark,
Jezebel.

Red light
For danger,
A nightmare of ages,
A madman's
Release
From his
Menopausal wife,
Jezebel.

How many men
Like ships in the night
Have passed you,
Harassed you,
Caressed you,
And paid you?
How many? How much?
Jezebel.

Simon Corby (15)

Observations of a Lavander Chic

The red and white beacons are the sharp pricks of
　　pain.
I strain my whole body to smile a smile of false
　　pretence.
Sorry for any delay said the little black man with the
　　shovel.
– All in the red triangle.
Countless concrete bridges,
Trusthouse Forte – A hamburger sir? fifty pounds.
Reduce speed now
Cheap travel and acme-reduced scenery
M6. Birmingham 72.
The cows wobble in their fields
Ford Long Vehicle.
Smoke, dust, spit, plastic.
Algi-spray.
Knutsford services –
Tea, Coffee, Micro-Technology and Plastic Surgery.
Pylons.
AA New Book of the Road.
The cool air strokes the hair on the back of my arm.
It's a motorway Mrs Robinson, sing Simon and
　　Garfunkel.
The highwaymen ride along on their white horses,
Armed robbery? A life sentence!
Carlsberg refreshes the parts other beers can't reach.
Scotties.
GB.
Ford again?
Splattered hedgehogs.
Tourist information and facilities for the disabled.
Slick gold wrist-watches
Hanimax
Let's all be patriotic.

All the lorries decked in their red, white and blue,
Long live the Queen!
('Who's that?') asked the tissue box.
RFV317X.
Mist,
More lamb. Mint sauce. Baa baa black sheep.
White lines,
Bee Gees.
Surprise
Woolworth
Catseyes
Wing mirror, winged mirrors.
Egg Shells
Hunger,
Perform Conditioner
Ringpull
Dr Peppers.
Beacons
Reduce speed.
Finished.

Andrew Wilson (13)

'Self Portrait'. Peter Cuthbert (14)

The Other Side of the Port

So this was what it was like;
Other side of the port.
The port was what
Separated
Life, where people lived,
From the life
That was just lived.
I could still see the
Neon lights,
Flashing,
And a vague sound
Of traffic and voices.
Whereas here everything was still;
Eerily so.
Yet I felt I was
Being watched,
Thousands
of eyes
    watching,
        staring,
Hostilely
Like natives.
It started raining
Hard,
I pulled my mac
Closer to me.
It somehow felt
Reassuring
To have something
        close.
On my side.
Well, now I'd seen it.
I guessed I'd better be
Heading for home.
Otherwise mum would start worrying.

But something;
What I don't know,
Compelled me to go on . . .
Into the debris surrounding
Derelict
Houses.
Homes?
I wasn't even
Sure
I wanted to know.
But still I went on.
Into a dead community.
There was an unpleasant
Lingery smell on the air,
Being blown
Like the rubbish
    on the
        wind,
Mingling with the
Stench
Of damp and decay.
The rain grew,
Harder.
I walked blindly on.
I felt like an insect
Caught,
In a spider's web.
There was, no return.
I started to run.
The feeling of glaring
Eyes became more intense.
I felt a bitter pang
Of regret and pity.
And a sharp taste of misery.
The web grew tighter.

Jocasta Clare Veda Brownlee (11)

City Life

Shouts and crowds, lights and music
fill the air as the night life begins.
The cold air carries the aroma of fish and chips.
Voices are heard as the fog laps round,
an uncontrolled fight.

'The Rat Race'. Matthew James (15)

Day breaks; men are rushing into offices and the Job
    Centre
is full up. Casual faces stroll on the drab concrete
    path.
Bargain hunters are queueing up outside shops.
A busy noise of traffic wafts into peoples' ears.

Jimmy Hargreves and his gang are playing Knock
    Down Ginger.
A bald head man is shouting, 'I'll kill you flipping
    nippers.'
Dark fumes from the factory and the school bell rings.

The afternoon comes. Police are dragging away
    shoplifters.
The final of the school marbles competition has
    begun.

Alan Jenkins (10)

City Centre

Crushed by the crowd
I tried to catch up with my Mum,
Trying to hold back the tears
Yet she wouldn't listen.

Cars roared
Engines snored
Never would I go again.
Tesco's peered over me as if it was alive
Riplon, Presto's and Preedy stared at me
Every step echoed.

Stephen Prior (10)

The Dump

The morning dew
Shines on the
Broken glass.
And the weeds
Struggle for survival
Between the
Cracks and slits
In the pavingstones.

The sun's beams
Gleam on an
Old bicycle frame
That is abandoned
And out of use.
The birds sing
In beautiful harmony
As another day begins.

Windblown newspapers
Roll about as
The wind blows,
And the day
Proceeds to
Lunch-time.
Fred's fish 'n' chip shop
Is at its best now.

The aroma of
The fish being
Fried and chips
Being deep-fried
Wafts out onto
The dump.
The car factory
Dumps scrap
Metal here once
A month.

The weeds open,
Open out into
Full bloom in
Mid' afternoon.
The dump now
Comes alive with
Adventurous children
Playing Tarzan in
The trees and
Sieving through the
Dump.

The sun sets
And children go
Home, the dump
Settles down for
The night.
The night scavengers
Come out for their
Prey as the night
Life begins.

Michael Barry Pickles (11)

Paper

Saturday night, and the city
is black and studded with lights
yellow, white and red
pavements throb and
the sky is lit up with a flash of neon
a symphony of drunken voices
can be heard, singing in tune with
the screech of car brakes
the smoky pubs, the discos, the sex joints
all are alive and breathing the Saturday night
air, all are shaking out their limbs,
cramped after a week of boredom
swept along by a sea of litter
towards the hungover dawn
lifted on their neon and vinyl
towards heaven, hell and the reaches beyond.

And what of the boy, the white and golden boy
who is staring, blank-faced with exhaustion
from his high window, over the city
towards the dark and silent lands beyond
his eyes glaze over
they are blue but
are as stony and cold as the white face
they are set in; they are so blue
you could see through them into
the blackness of his skull
were it not for the blank screen
kept invariably behind them

'Banana Pencil', Paul Cronshaw (13)

Childishly, he is crying
as he surveys his city
his ink-stained, wiry fingers,
their nails bitten down to the quick,
grasp the catch on the grimy window
and push it open
for a moment the raw-nerved, red-eyed boy
lets the cool air in
to rid himself of the stale silence

Seconds later some crumpled grubby
sheets of paper
are thrown out on the breeze
they float gently,
rise, and are carried by
the hushed wind
out into the graveyard darkness.

Emma Payne (15)
(Highly commended)

Pub Light

Smoke tendrils,
Boa constriction of fumes
Unfiltered.
Heavy, wasted passage
Of unspoken tedium.
A humid companionship,
And the comforting hubbub
Of broken phrases.
A grizzled jumper
Hunched over a pint.
Flotillas
Of frothy, crystal glasses,
On fretted beer-mats.
The drawn parabola
Of a swinging door
Emits chilled segments
Of crisp invigoration.
Light bursts in shafts,
Arrowing the mustiness.
Outside,
Solicitude.

Janet Rowse (16)

The Ghost Town

In the ghost town, the phantoms lurk in the
Dusty streets.
In the ghost town, the phantom sherriff guards
The murky city.
In the ghost town, the phantom barmaid
Serves the phantoms in the smoky saloon.

In the ghost town, the phantom clerk looks
After the desolate bank.
In the ghost town, the phantom grocer makes
His sullen deliveries.
In the ghost town, the phantom jailer makes
Ghastly faces at the sad prisoners.
In the ghost town, the phantom farmer takes
Care of the transparent animals.
In the ghost town, the phantom postman
Puts the sealed letters through the broken doors.

Andrew Robert Shave (10)

Life in East Berlin?

6. 15 a.m.
I woke to hear a gunshot,
Murdering the silence of dawn.
I looked out
Of my uncurtained window
To see a guard
On the wall
Aim
And take another shot.
I followed the line of his fire –
Some poor bastard
Was lying in the river
Dying,
Then the shot
That he would never hear
Killed me
A little more.

Roy Biddle (14)
(Highly commended)

83

Escape!

9 a.m., early morning
Prisoners sleeping, captors yawning.

The prisoners awake
But no noise do they make.
For this is the day
They're going away.

Back to their lovers,
Their sisters, their brothers,
Back to their homeland
So dear to their hearts.

No one can stop them,
The tunnel is ready,
Nervous, excited and rather unsteady.

Usually the mornings are uncontrollably violent
But this morning is different – everything's silent.

Never before has there been a silence so long,
The captors suspect that something is wrong.

They search the whole ground,
But nothing is found,
And still from the prisoners comes not a sound.

All look so tired, withering in shape,
It's hard to be believe that tonight they'll escape.

They total a number of thirty-three
Who crawl out of the tunnel, escape and are free.

Five arrive home, sweaty and hot,
The others are caught, lined up and shot.

Richard Gadd (14)

Bus Stop

A humped-up bundle of clothes
And a shopping basket, almost empty,
A withered lady sits chewing her gums.
A freckled-faced girl leans across her friend,
A pimply boy lights her cigarette;
Laughing they mimic the withered lady.
Slouching she fumbles for a cigarette,
Her NHS glasses, brown, horn-rimmed
Slide slowly down her wrinkled nose.
The girl hits the boy and swears
Then laughs as the boy hits back.
Crumpled and faded like her face,
Her coat is draped over her.
She sucks slowly on a mint
And coughs hoarsely till her eyes water.
The girl and her friends stand up.
The bus shudders to a halt.
They flick away their ash as if
Flicking away the memory
Of that lonely lady.

Bryony Corner (14)

An Old Derelict Station

The lonely old station was still,
There was a slight chill in the air,
A rusty sign said 'Park Hill',
But otherwise it was bare.

There were weeds penetrating the platform,
And thistles here and there,
The room where folk once waited in the warm,
Was now beyond repair.

A layer of dust covered the bench,
Stuffing dangled out of a tear,
The atmosphere was a mouldy stench,
And the skirting, a spider's lair.

The building itself was derelict,
Which gave a sense of despair,
Mildew and moss were in conflict,
Ivy hung off the wall like hair.

Patrick Humphris (10)

The Road

My head is in the country
With the sheep and cattle.
My arms are in the village
As the cobble stones.
My stomach is in the town
With the shops and flats.
My legs are in the city
With the buses and lorries.
I meet different people,
I've seen the new Sierra,
I take you home from school,
I stretch onwards for ever and ever.

Janet Ticer (10)

Destruction

Saxon Road,
 once a beautiful place.
But now,
 a dump.
Gardens were inhabited
 by roses, carnations,
 crocuses and,
 later, snowdrops.
No more though,
 only weeds and rubbish
 exist in the gardens of Saxon Road now.
As I walk through London Street,
 it is the same.

The same misery,
　　the same disgusting smell of cats.
The same doors on
　　the same broken, rusty hinges.
The same shattered glass,
　　in the same broken frames,
With peeling paint and splintered,
　　rotten wood.
The once immaculately carved statues
　　have been broken
　　and scattered everywhere.
I hear a cat and a dog,
　　both rather scrawny, fighting
　　and overturning dustbins.
Then, paper and cardboard,
　　and tin and other rubbish
　　roll towards me like tumbleweed.
Down the road,
　　a demolition gang is at work,
And rounding the corner I see,
　　and hear,
The crashing of bricks,
The shattering of glass
And the snapping of rotted wood.
An almost tangible misery;
　　a misery that is in the weather;
　　a cold, hard misery,
　　like the biting frost and
　　the strong, cruel winds of today,
　　is in the air.
The wind blows to me the smell of stale air,
　　and, as I inhale,
I find the choking taste of brick dust
　　in my throat and eyes.

Further along the road
    and down two alleyways
    is a church.
I cautiously enter by way of a large,
    oak door.
It groans.
I walk along the aisle,
    and I hear ghostly voices singing in the pews.
And, as I listen I am in the year 1940,
    singing merrily.
Then the song is over,
I sit down and watch
    the Bishop conducting a church service.
Then, the siren, the air raid siren,
Screaming, everyone rushes for cover
    but I was too late and was hit!
I shake myself and as I look
    up I see a stained glass window,
    broken beyond repair.
Obviously the gang was at work again.
A large ball of weight
    had gone through the window.
Time I wasn't here.
I slam the door shut,
    but – no,
    must've been that crane again!
I rush away,
    away from the melancholy church.
Away from London Street,
Away from Saxon Road,
Away, away, away.

Louise Ann Bashford (11)
(Highly commended)

Beirut – A Day in the Death of

*(To those of the Sabra and Chatila camps, alive and
   dead, hoping that nothing similar will happen
   again)*

> Life stirred –
> The sun rose, birds sang.

The soldier shifted slightly,
Stretched and yawned, leant
His gun against his other shoulder.

> Behind the crumbling wall
> Smiling, shrill-voiced mothers called.
> Playing happily,
> Their children wouldn't come.
> Seven ages chattered, cried;
> All seven ages to be destroyed.

The soldier coughed, his throat gone dry . . . But
He spoke a different language,
Wouldn't hear their pleas, when he let
That army in among them,
Like hunting hounds unleashed.

A movement in the corner of his eye,
Lorries, driving slowly, crowded faces,
Guns.   A sight he would deny.
They marched towards
The open gates,
The talking, trusting people.
Just keeping order – no biblical sin –
He reassured his conscience.
Nausea rising, he turned away.

90

Inside, a job was being done;
Knives flashed, guns flared.
Initial reluctance being passed
One can murder methodically;
It can be done with no feeling,
The manual had said,
Forgetting to mention
The long, drawn-out screams.
Some run, some fight,
Concealing fear and hatred.
Bodies pile up. The sun goes down.
Spotlights flood the camp,
Leaving no dark corners to hide.
The soldiers scribble graffiti
With knives; on bodies.
Mothers, babies,
Both are slaughtered.
On into the night . . .
Eyes glazed, he saw his future:
Discussion of his case –
Shellshock, you know. We cannot
Understand. He only witnessed
Extermination of laughing, living people.
Again the sun rose –
Red as blood –
Nothing stirred.

Lara Burns (15)
(Highly commended)

The Death of Ireland (Bloody Sunday)

Crimson lace seeping from
    the death of a man,
Chalk-white in his innocence.
Around him the sound of gunfire
Ricochets off scarred walls;
While sheep in red-faced confusion
(Having run into khaki
Like lambs to the slaughter),
Scatter from a riddled grave.

A doctor bending over a corpse
Momentarily freezes –
As a child screams.

Shrouded figures gaze:
Transfixed:
As a woman,
(Hysterical at the feet of
    her husband),
Sheds bitter tears of religious hate.

While, black and white against the
    stage,
A priest sighs,
As he closes the frozen eyelids
Of an unknown martyr.
And, cursing the killers under his breath;
Realizes, that with death
Comes the stripping of
    religious barriers;
And, asking for the help of
    a Protestant nun,
Moves the body to a
    bomb-shelled house;
Where, for once unifying
    Ireland,
They administer last rites.

Charlotte Cook (16)
(Highly commended)

'The Toy Shop', Philip Beglan (10)
(Highly commended)

Poem Written after a Visit to the Sweet Shop at Blists Hill Museum, Telford

Old fashioned
Sweet shop, covered
In tiles guarding the
Counter for years.
Old, gas lights
Shining bright
Giving light for years and years.
Old door, hungry children
Opening the door for years.
Old scales, been rocking
About by sweets for years.
I liked the smell
In the sweet shop
And I hope children have
For years.

Edward James (7)

Seasons

All Seasons

Snow tops the mountain
Pink blossom is on the trees
Fresh green grass begins to grow
Lambs frisk about the fields,
Spring has come.

Patches of snow are on the mountain
Cherries ripen on the trees
Grass shows dew on the top
Lambs explore the hills,
Summer has come.

The mountain is covered by a mist
Leaves fall off the trees
Grass turns brown under the harvest moon
Sheep stay close to one another,
Autumn has come.

Snow covers the mountain
The trees are left quite bare
Grass is covered with sleet and ice
Sheep are safe in the barn,
Winter has come.

All seasons have come and gone,
They will show themselves again.

Katherine Quinn (8)

Nonsense

Put on your bathing suits in December,
In summer warm furry clothes remember,
June winds coming from the South,
Put a scarf over your mouth,
April showers at the end of May,
This will complete your nonsense day.

Joanne Allen (13)

Autumn's Beginning

The leaves rustle through the air,
With every plum a wasp is there,
Autumn time is here again.
Sometimes wind and sometimes rain
Birds are singing in the tree,
Look at them no they can't catch me.
Rustle, rustle, golden-browny red
Settle down, pretty ones, settle down to bed.
The leaves are crunchy
And they are all so bunchy,
Autumn is here come out to play
This is one of a lovely day.

Carla Spray (7)

'A Lowry Street', Angela Griffiths (7)

November

A thousand diamonds joined together on the
     common.
Ice sparkles in the Autumn sun.
A frosty smell, almost indescribable,
A rim of ice round each pebble.
A nippy time of the year, when the frost nips
     you like small fingers.
Leaves scatter out of the trees, leaving them
     almost bare.
Trees themselves are tangling their branches
     together, like a mass of witches' hair.
The pale blue sky seems to whine for warmer
     weather.

Ailsa McNaughton (7)

Autumn

The early morning mist soon clears,
The cobwebs, like silver, shimmer in the pale
    morning sunlight.
A light breeze catches the leaves and sends
Them whirling in a shower of golden brown to the
    damp earth below.
White smoke curls upwards from the chimney pots
And dewdrops glisten on the grass.
There is a touch of frost in the air
And children hurry to school to keep warm,
Their scarves and gloves making a bright splash
    of colour.
The hedgerows are aglow with red berries
And the holly leaves shine as though they had been
    polished.
All is clean and fresh,
But how still everything is before the
Icy grip of winter steals in.

Richard Hodgson (11)

The Conker

I felt in my pocket for a small, spherical shape.
I drew it out, by its string, and thought hard.
Gradually my mind moved to another place;
It was a forest, with chestnut trees,
Boys shouting, climbing trees,
The swishing of water, girls splashing in it,
Tree houses, rope swings and several rafts,
But then 'Crack!', and as I looked down,
I saw the remnants of a conker, on a boot-lace.

Peter Conlong (11)

Autumn

The clear blue sky is sunny,
But the sun's warmth is not felt.
A smoky thin mist covers the ground,
Hiding a white morning frost.
Chestnuts, limes and silver birches
Are all a yellowy brown.
A rustling crunch of leaves underfoot
Leads me to a small hill.
Over the hill seems to be a volcano,
With countless drops of larva
Flying in red, orange, yellow and brown.
Nearby is a holly bush,
With sharp green leaves,
And a thousand small red eyes.

Peter Conlong (11)

The Autumn Nightfall

The Autumn night is coming.
Darkness dawns at six o'clock.
The sky is greyening.
Late birds twitter,
Short, sharp notes slicing through the air.
Angry black grey cumuli.
It drifts windedly across a fierce sky.
The barening trees shuffle their branches,
Dark silhouettes against the grey, dusky sky.
Squares of light illuminate the dark, shadowy
　　　houses.
Two beaming circles at the front of each motor-
　　　powered beetle.
They pick out a way through a forest of gloomy
　　　buildings.
Oblong lights outline the shape of a monster
　　　bus.
An eerie screech befalls a slow Autumn
　　　scrounger;
The hedgehog.
His companion squeaks and shuffles, searching
　　　bewilderedly.
A scattering of fended birds marks the fall
　　　of the evening.
One plain, dark cloud now masses over the sky,
Blocking all dusk's last light.
The swirling blanket waits to burst.
It hangs lower and lower.
First a slithering spatter,
Then a harder rain.
At last the cloud is rewarded,
It pours out the burden;
A sleety Autumn rain.

The roads are flooded in the outpour.
Revenge has beaten the sun's tempest.
The Autumn night is now a bedraggled world of
    shadows.

Nicola Chapman (11)

Autumn

In the northern hemisphere
Down they fall with little fear.

A hundred, a thousand
All over a mountain.

In a town
And on a plain.

On the sand
And in the fountain.

Down they fall
Down, down, down.

Large leaves, small leaves,
Short leaves, tall.

Red and green,
Yellow and Brown.

From the trees in threes
They fall.

Leaves fall, even when green
On to branches and in between.

Pointed leaves and round
All over the ground.

Leaves on the grass
Get blown as I pass.

Branches and trees are bare
When into the distance I stare.

Elantha Evans (7)

A Hard Winter

All the world is covered in snow,
It's so very cold and there's nowhere to go,
No birds sing, no flowers grow
Hunger hurts and the wind does blow.

The beggars limp round dirty bins,
The dogs lick meat from empty tins,
Brothers in hunger no warmth, no cheer,
Their backs to the wind while winter's here.

But don't despair for spring is there,
Waiting to bring back the weather fair,
Then berries will bloom for mile after mile
The plants will grow and people will smile.

Karen Kirkpatrick (7)

102

The Window

Gazing out onto the winter scene
At slated roofs draped, and shrouded.
Hopeful child curled up like a weary slumbering
      kitten at the window.
Bright eyed at the wonder of winter.

Dancing flakes cascading, an avalanche of snow
      to cover the window sill
Sprinkling powder like icing sugar upon a cake
And transforming greenery into a silvery glow.

Trees become skeleton-like figures, throwing
    shadowy reflections on the garden path
Struggling figures breathing cool vapours into the
    freezing air
While gardens desolate, the neglected snowmen
    silently stand.

The rhythmic mirage of dancing flakes
Lulls the child's sleep-laden eyes,
Dreamlike he turns to the welcoming hearth
Where dancing flames envelope him in a rosy glow.

Scott Lowis (14)

The Snowman

He stood alone,
In the dark out there,
The ground was white,
And the trees were bare.

The wind blew hard,
The snow swirled round,
So cold he looked,
Yet he made no sound.

How glad I was,
To be inside,
By the warm soft glow,
Of the fireside.

Joanne Allen (13)

The Cold Morning

The bleached landscape below was dismal.
Cold, transparent daggers were poised, ready to kill.
The occasional early riser cultivated the snow.
The snow was blown around like an icy sandstorm,
The dunes were blocking the road.
The river was as motionless as a statue,
Yearning to break loose.
A shiver ran down my spine,
And I climbed back into bed.

Peter Conlong (11)

Snow

Snow is as white as a snowbird's wing.
Down the bird flies, and he sits upon a tree.

Snow is as white as a pure white horse.
Down the horse runs, galloping by.

The snow is as white as a white fluffy pillow.

Snow is as dazzling as a white butterfly, down it flies,
    and softly flies away.

Deepak Gupta (8)

'Snow', Lee Homer Dob (9)

Snow

The snow comes,
The ground is now a little white carpet,
Children build snowmen,
Big, white ghosts –
Cuddly but cold.

Rhian Evans (8)

Hail

The hail comes,
A whip of ice,
Cruelly wielded by a raging cloud
Thrashing the earth below.

Rajeev D. S. Raizada (10)

Colder Days

Dismal, colourless fields.
Black skeletons of trees dotted on the horizon.
A lacy spider's web hangs from a shed door.
Frosted patterns on the windows.
The sky is an icy blue.
The black silhouette of a bird crosses the sky.
Colourless, bleak winter.

Kim Woodsford (8)

The Doom of December

Why
Must the year
End now
At the final day
Of the
Month?

Two
Endings
At once
Is like double murder
To the
Calendar.

It's
A heartless
Thing to
Do. 'Happy New Year'
Really
Means
   The
      End.

Kate Haworth (10)

Snowdrop

I met a little woman,
Swaying in the breeze,
She was a little snowdrop,
I thought that she might freeze.
Then I saw many more,
Clustered all around.
Green stalks, white petals,
Crouching on the ground.
My little snowdrop women,
Gossiping all day,
Their time is passing fast now,
They'll wither all away.
Then we'll meet again next year
To talk another day.

Elinor Hudson-Davies (7)

Snowdrops . . .

Each simple bud is delicately formed,
And each vein is like a velvet seam,
As though they had been sewn together with
Invisible stitches.

The outside petals droop,
Like the ears of a rabbit
And each tear-like flower is unafraid of
Outside dangers.
They are very bold and brave
On a cold morning when,
The frost captures them
With a crystal shield.

Elizabeth Ham (10)

The First Primrose

I saw the primrose,
While I was walking down the lane,
Tucked under the hedges,
Delicate and fragile,
The petals were yellow, as a small sun,
Velvety, smooth and soft.

Wrinkled leaves,
Curly around the edges.
Deeply veined,
Green as grass,
It tells you like a messenger,
That Spring is on its way.

Mark Goble (11)

Cherry Blossom

Delicate petals
Fall gently to the ground,
A pink floor of beauty.

Clair Inston (10)

The Oak

Acorn
tiny, hidden
living, germinating, growing
shoot, roots – trunk, branches
swaying, blossoming, towering
sturdy, mighty
Oak

Stuart Little (14)

'Summer Trees'. Andrew Lee (11)

Summer in the 'Old Days'

We would sprawl lavishly on the lawn,
Consuming thinly spread sandwiches, home-made
   jam,
Then lick our fingers,
Until we could taste nothing but dirt.
After a slice of apple pie, we would play cricket,
Until the sun scorched our backs,
And we could play no more,
But just sit and let the muck in the gutters
Sieve through our hands, like a waterfall,
Or lie on the lawn chewing thin stalks of grass.
Later we would depart and go our separate ways,
Back to the mundane old street, with the same
   houses,
That stood in a row, the same children,
Playing the exact games they had been playing
When we left that morning, chicken with a water
   balloon,
Shrieking and yelling when sodden,
Like the pebbles scream on the beach
When the tide covers them;
Using their wet, dusty hands, they would wipe away
The sweat beads which dripped into their eyes.

Joanne Edwards (15)

Sonnet to Weeds

In each and every corner of the earth,
Beside the fine and honoured sovereign plants
Are those whose aspect is awarded mirth
For they have not yet joined the hot-house dance.
Our garden beauties wear a constant guise
Wrought by men disillusioned – wanting gain;
The weeds find their taint from what we devise,
From compulsion thriving off neglect and rain.
From dazzling impressions we are so prone
To cast out weeds and for hybrids settle,
Can lily, like comfrey ease bruised, broken bone?
To cleanse the blood, what cheaper than nettle?
So why should we think weeds a trouble brought?
For once 'wild, untamed' the rose was thought.

Clare Griffiths (13)

Making a Red Rose

Take a few tears,
From a sad clown's face.
Squeeze the colour
Out of a ruby.
Dip the tears into the colour,
And there you have the petals.

Stitch the petals together,
With the thread
Of a money spider.
The rose begins to take its form

Weave a strip of green cotton,
From the plants of South America
Attach on either side,
The sharpnesses of many wasps' stings.
Stick the head to the stem,
With the resin of a willow.
   There you have a red rose.

Joanne Cater (12)

The Rose Petal

So frail, so delicate was the intricate design
of the rose petal

Lying there below the trees whispering in the
twinkling twilight

Entangled in autumn leaves orange, red, gold . . .

Joining in the game of rushing around in circles of
   wind

Then slowly floating down into the depths
of the leaves.

Katie Hillier (11)

Mushroom Field

The little corner of our field
There the best mushrooms grow,
Light brown tops like heads
    of bald men.

Curling round to the brown
    underneath
Frilled like the air compartment
    of a concertina
The stem,
Long fat big as a finger:

Pulling the mushroom,
Breaking the hair-fine roots,
Piled in the little bag,
    getting only the ripest
Saving the rest for
    next harvest.

Kristian Heal (12)

The Country Sleuth

The cows are feasting on the soft flourishing grass,
Whence the metaphysic farmer orders them to
    march.
They clatter slowly up the farmyard, into the parlour
    above.

The elegant cocks crow, roosting on a fence.
Facing each other in a coat of arms,
Heralds of splendour.
Their cry as sharp as an axe of light.
The performance of the tractor splutters through a
    field,
Lacerating grass for the Winter's store.
Night falls fiercely when quartered moon is pale:
Tawny owl scans for pathetic prey.

Malcolm Caldwell (13)

A Hot Summer Evening

I stand on the steps, with a cup of water in my hand,
And watch the swifts circling and screaming
    overhead.
I think of the Siamese cat who came to the garden
Wandering.
I went out to caress the beautiful creature
The slim, oriental shadow . . .
But it was shy and wary, untrusting and seemed
    lost and could not get out.
And so I opened the carport door and I went back
    into the garden to show it that it was not a trap.

115

'Sunflower'. Nicola Dobson (7)

Yet still it hesitated
Could it not get down from the wall?
No, it was just considering, testing each step, and
    finally
It jumped and went out.
But not quickly
And as I went to close the door it was a small way
        down the lane
It stopped and looked at me . . .
Blue eyes
I think I have caught a glimpse of a god.

Ruth Leader (13)

The Natural World

Sunrise

Suddenly the brown match-like trees
    have dyed easterly branches;
Their amber points move noiselessly with the wind.
Quiet ripples come from the head of the sheltering
  mountain,
    right up, now to the stone's edge.
They loll up over their jagged points,
    lapping away the jadeness with their hungry
  tongues.
Silently, gloom breaks, filtering out the sun;
The acid breath of dawn breaks through.
Light pours through the ragged
clouds –
Where does the gloom depart to?
A golden beam of sunlight spreads over
    the shimmering country, lighting up the earth.
The glistening water shivers,
Pronouncing thousands of tiny golden diamonds.
The speckled mountains, filtered shadows,
The splendour of light is proclaimed.
    The world is astir.

Daphne Curry (13)

117

Sunset

There's the sun going down over
    the water.
Orange light glows, twinkling, shimmering and
    sparkling,
Flickering everywhere, glowing on
    the shimmering water,
Silhouetting everything around.
The roads are like yellow crystal
While the red and orange sky glows.
Then the sun fades in the water.
Darkness comes.

Angela Nicholls (7)

The Garden

An imaginary wonderland
With red roses rambling up long ruined walls,
Silver dew resting on emerald green blades,
And forget-me-nots opening their bright petals in
    the early sunshine.

Primroses bursting into full bloom
As the first rays touch the forgotten lawns,
The bright colours of sunrise breathe new
    life upon the long-lost garden –
The fallen fence, the path covered with sprays
    of bramble,
And a white streak of daisies.

Emily Pivonka (7)
(Highly commended)

A Stroll along the Seaside

The smell of the sea tingles in my nose,
As I walk along the sea front.
I can see such things as a spade soiled by the sand,
Stones all round and smooth,
Shifting sand gathering like camels' humps;
As these humps grow, turn to desolate dunes.

To the rocky part now,
Where I can see limpets stuck fast,
As if they were sucking the rock,
Crabs hiding in rocky crags,
And waves crashing in rock crevices,
Then falling back into the swaying, shivering sea.

Mark Davis (11)

'Pirate Treasure', Simon Sobhani (11)

High Tide

The tide rushes in, then it falls
The wind is whistling then it calls
To the mossy harbour walls
    And the docks
The waves are crashing on the shore.
The grey seals hear a deafening roar
While over them the seagulls soar
    From the rocks
Here you see the sleek seals play
On the sandbank in the bay,
Splashing each other in the spray
    Having fun.
Here you see a crab keep cool,
Bathing in a rocky pool.
Pebbles sparkle just like jewels
    In the sun.
In a cranny sparkling bright
Where you see the stars at night
A golden starfish reflects the light
    As he lolls.
Out at sea the herring glide.
While the mackerel try to hide
From fishing boats in the high tide
    With their trawls.
Little new born wavelets bring
Mussels, cockles and whelks that cling
To build a throne for the sea king
    In the sea.
Fishermen in boats go by
And hang their big nets out to dry.
While clouds make patterns in the sky
    Just for me.

Margaret Bell (7)
(Highly commended)

The Brine

The place for me,
Is not the sea.
Not when I think,
That I might sink.
Another thing,
Jellyfish sting.
And crabs have claws.
And sharks have jaws.
Out in the sun,
The waves look fun.
But underneath,
Are horrid teeth!

Fred Woods (11)

The Rain is my Friend

The rain is my friend
I love splashing about
And playing at Pooh-sticks
All by myself.

The rain is my friend
I love watching the drops
As they run down the pane,
Or shine in the rainbow
High in the sky.

The rain is my friend
I love walking along,
Under my umbrella
Watching the drops
As they bounce up from the ground.

The rain is my friend,
I love being wet
But why will nobody play with me
Till it's sunny again?

Karla Nelson (8)

It's Raining

The first gentle patters on the windowpane,
As the crying begins,
Then lashed with the winds of anger,
A down-pouring rage.
Helpless trees shivering,
Bathed in cold misery.
Obscured, greyed hills,
Lonely without the sun's warmth.
Sadness and creeping melancholy,
And then the drip, drip, drip,
Of wasted tears.

Clare Johnson (16)

The Wind

The wind is a herd of antelopes.
Galloping quite near me,
But not quite on top of me
Thundering past.
The speed of their run,
Brushing me.

As they touch the grass,
It shakes underneath them,
Making a hollow noise
On the ground.
The trees whistle and shake
In fear of the thousands
And millions of antelopes
Trampling the earth
To dust.

Sarah Lee (10)

A Mad Storm

A raving storm
Is like a mad dragon
Clashing its teeth
Beating its tail
Slashing with its great silver claws.
Lightning flashes from its blood-red eyes
And a smile on its bloodstained face.
Then – suddenly a Knight appears
Dressed in a light-blue armour
On a great blue stallion.
He charges suddenly
His lance sinks deep
And all is silent.
The storm has halted
The dragon is killed.

Mark Roscoe (10)

The Thunderstorm

The afternoon heat glared on the fields,
The ground parched and desperate,
The sky dark blue and a haze
Hanging like a blanket over the horizon.

Then, on the horizon
A small insignificant cloud
Nothing first but then growing
Increasing, expanding, darkening and shrouding the
    sun.

Then comes the first faint rumbling of thunder,
The rumbling increases,
The heavens open,
The rain pours down,
The lightning fractures the storm clouds in two
Then the thunder peals
Splitting the sky with an enormous roll of drums.

The lightning strikes again,
Like a momentary fissure in a plateau of storm
    clouds,
Immediately the thunder explodes
Like a thousand bombs in quick succession,
Shattering the sky.

Charles Lovett-Turner (12)

After the Storm

The sea is calm,
Everywhere is hushed,
There's a gentle stillness
Where the waves once rushed,
The beach is deserted,
Though the sun smiles down,
As if it has pity,
On the wet and dreary town.

Sonia Bowen (13)

A Journey over Swallow Falls

Silent at first, chattering gently,
Over the wet, shiny stones.
Then it begins to race a little faster,
Rushing and gushing along.

The pulse begins to beat more loudly
The water raises its voice,
It has to go on now, further and further,
Because it has no choice.

Now is the moment! It leaps from the rock
And darts like a swallow in flight.
Then crashes down to the rapids below,
A whirlpooling, turbulent fight.

Yet again and again it tumbles down,
Foaming and bubbling white.
The spray flies high in the air
And the rocks are sparkling bright.

The water begins to slow down
And all the excitement is gone,
Then very quietly and gently,
The water flows on . . .

Lisa Anscomb (12)

Reflections in the River

The buildings hung in the blue water,
A fish swam in and out of the windows.
A face of a wrinkled boy peered over,
A tadpole swam in his hair and hid up his nose.
The sky down there rippled slowly.
Different shapes of white floated by.
The boy waved at himself in the water,
The wrinkled boy waved back at him,
And a plane swam upside down.

Adam Gilson (13)
(Highly commended)

'My Brother',
Iain Sturrock (14)

How Strange

How strange . . .
While wet snow falls,
The daffodils bloom.

The sky is blank. Emotionless. Concealing secrets.
I sit watching from the window.
The daffodils are fresh clear cut and the
    surroundings blurred, out of focus.

A bird flies across the sky
Quickly, it wants to get into shelter.
It doesn't fit into the picture
Too fast, too fast,
The rest is slow, asleep
A moment frozen in time

Strange . . .

Ruth Leader (13)
(Highly commended)

A Lighted Candle

The
flame,
A gentle creature,
A spark of innocent life:
A delicate, flickering spirit,
Licking, tasting, slender and
Stretching, gracefully glowing,
Rosily reaching . . . greedily
Feeding on hollow wax, powerfully
Casting infinite shadows,
Breaking the shell of darkness.
Destructive tongue of flame,
One puff and a bellow
Of scattered twisting,
Turning smoke
Grey. Dull.
Dead.

Duncan Boswell (13)

Candlelight

As darkness pours into the world,
Like coffee into cup,
With silver stars to sweeten,
The Gods begin to sup.

As children softly dream away,
Their rainbow fantasies,
Of prince and pauper, tramp and king,
Of birds and honey bees.

As owl raises his weary head,
And blinks his wise old eyes,
He shakes his wings and soars away,
With weird and ghost-like cries.

As angels guard o'er weary heads,
And see that all is right,
My wax, white sentinel of the night –
My candle, burns so bright.

The upright flame of white and gold,
The velvet vision true,
The golden pool of perfect light,
That every night seems new.

My candle burns while this I write,
I feel its kindly glow,
I feel the thrill of old, lost days,
I never am to know.

I feel the sense of perfect calm,
Of stories I have read,
The treasured books upon the shelf,
Are stored within my head.

The candlelight has seen all this,
Seen poets come and go,
Seen many midnight writers try
To let their feelings show.

To share the thoughts of eventide,
To share the thoughts of night,
To scribble down the magic thrill,
Of mellow candlelight.

J. Lamerton (13)

Burning

The match was struck,
It snatched its prey,
And slowly the paper
Began to curl and scorch.
The corner crumbled away,
As the flame rushed on
Devouring the pure white paper.

It danced and ran, twisting
And turning, then leaping high
In the air.
The hungry flame raced
Onwards.
Leaving red-flecked ash
Slowly drifting downwards.
Now nothing was left but a
Whisp of smoke and a
Faint lingering smell in the air.

Suzy Gilmour (11)

The Night of the Ebony Moon

Dark is the sky and dark is the Earth
On the night of the ebony moon.
Fearsome the ways and evil the deeds
When the dark night comes to its noon.

Silent, the cat as it pads on the roof,
Through a dismal and visionless world.
Unseen is the wakeful and hunting bat
With its velvety wings unfurled.

Loud is the bark of a distant dog,
Disturbing the sombre calm.
Faint is the light at the foot of the hill,
From a lonely and much-weathered farm.

Speckled with stars is the cloth of the night,
Though daylight will cover it soon.
Feeble, those battling pinpoints of light,
Resisting the dark of the moon.

Elaine Campbell (13)

Diamond

Rock
dull, rough
scraping, weathering, shattering
lumps, pebbles – shapes, light
cutting, polishing, gleaming
bright, expensive
Diamond

Stuart Little (14)

The Moor

The ground damp beneath my feet,
The mist touching everything with
      cold, icy fingers,
The dark horizon outlined by the bleak
      sky
Bracken unfurls and throws out tiny
      seeds, popping as it does so.
The distant melancholy melody of a dawn
      bird.
Peace, silence.
The trees stand bare against the
      greyness,
Crimson and gold leaves flutter about the
      ground in the sighing breeze,
Rocks, and boulders stand out in
      the darkness of the morn
My heart throbs in the loneliness
Loneliness . . . that yet, is not lonely.
A strange feeling inside bursting to
      get out.
Happiness and joy fill me.
Many things are beautiful but
      none more so as here,
Nature beauty, Nature's love to share
      with all.
I could sit here forever, forever on
      the moors.

Karen Thomas
(Highly commended)

The Fog Witch

The fog is weary,
Creeping and crawling,
In and out,
Backwards and forwards.
It seems like a creepy witch to me,
Hiding in the bushes,
Making spells.
She waves her wand from side to side,
Saying her magic words,
And smoky fog floats from the pot,
Twirling and swirling in the murky air
With swishing sounds
And settling on the sleeping houses.

Jessica Adler (7)

The Fog Serpent

Creeping, advancing
Licking my face with its long clammy
Tongue.
Enclosing me in its grey arm,
Deceiving me by opening its reaching
Tentacles yet closing them ahead
Again.
Ruffling its smooth but damp scales
Against my legs.
Loitering, lingering yet moving
Slowly, laying its mysterious
Body over me,
Whiskers blurring the lamp light
Ahead,
A serpent sliding on its way.

Kathryn Light (11)

Morning

The flower heads hang heavily
As the bee swims inside.
Sun has just risen,
Night has just died;
Outside in the garden,
An awful sound is heard,
An early worm is eaten,
By an early bird.

Stuart Bage (11)

Night

Slowly the sunlight is stamped out
As the giant called Darkness
Creeps over the land and sea.
So silently he heaves his great body
Over the sleepy or drowsy earth.
Already his spell has settled on
The people and beasts living on the earth.
Soon darkness has filled every crack in
     every corner in every home.
But as soon as the world is flooded with
     darkness
It is flooded also with fear
And a longing for light.
So the giant moves on.
And leaves the earth to be taken by the
     sun.
For a while.

Luciana O'Flaherty (11)

Night

I am Night,
Black as soot,
Down from the sky,
Switching on street lights,
Scaring children,
My name – Night.

I am Night,
I feel still,
Cold as ice,
A black cloudy face,
Like nothing on earth,
My name – Night.

I am Night,
Moving slowly,
Car headlights peer into my gloom,
Breaking my body,
Swords of light,
Lights – my enemy.

I am Night,
Lord of darkness,
Enemy of light,
I create shadows,
To scare you,
Lights – my enemy.

I am Night,
Maker of bumps in the night
Howling winds
Like wolves,
Also my creation,
Sounds – my servants.

Daniel Thompson (9)

The Moon Mare

The moon comes out at night, shining brightly,
A bright beam shoots down to earth,
Suddenly a horse appears,
She is the Moon Mare.
She creates terror in the neighbourhood,
Her strange shape gallops through the towns,
One night, the townspeople make a plan,
They will capture the Moon Mare.
The townspeople go up behind her with a rope,
They throw it over her head,
It touches her,
She vanishes,
The strange beam comes back to earth,
Slowly, you see her shadow disappearing to the
      moon,
The beam disappears,
Silence . . .

Fiona Gibson (11)

The Angry Man

He is an angry man,
His seething stomach rumbling
      like distant thunder,
The whole earth trembles
      at the sight of him,
uprooting young trees,
overturning soil and stones.
Stifled temper wells up
      and slowly takes its grip,
         swelling beyond control.

Then with a sudden outburst of fury –
    sweltering, searing, scorching,
He runs wild,
    wrenching at large trees,
    battering down doors
    as he flares through his village.
He lashes in molten rage
    at everything within reach,
hurling it high into the air . . .

. . . At length,
    his violence spent,
He staggers with exhaustion
      gasping for breath.

Sweaty steam
    rises from his feverish body
    and fills the air,
    turning to water
    and raining poison-sulphur
Over the little which has survived
    Until . . .

. . . Nothing is left.
The desolation of death
    pollutes the atmosphere
      for miles
around that huge exhausted bulk,
for the angry man . . .
    . . . is a volcano.

Nicola Jane Field (10)

Animals

Death on Velvet Paws

Eyes,
Like stars,
In a sea of black,
Soft fur.
The gentle 'pad pad'
Of paws.
Teeth as sharp as knives.
Claws,
Like pearly daggers,
Sheathed in velvet gloves.
Deadly hunter with gleaming eyes
Searching,
Searching the darkness for anything,
Anything alive.
Crouching low,
He stalks forward,
Then pounces,
Claws extended.
A shriek of pain,
Then silence.
Death
Wins

Fiona Skiera (13)

Harris and the Swan

Harris dives to the water,
Lands on the swan. Plop.
He doesn't want to hurt it,
Only play,
But like a big white Li-lo
He cannot sink it.
The white wings
Spread over the water,
I run, run, run
Calling 'Dad, Dad!'
I am wet, wet with splashing.
I feel better,
Dad is now there,
Calling Harris off the white wonder,
Harris, his fur ruffled, slinks back to Dad.
The swan shakily swims off.
The tremendous fight over.

Matthew Watson (10)
(Highly commended)

The White Stallion

The white stallion
Stands
At the far end
Of the meadow
Hoof high
In thick green grass.
He's always there
A solitary, mysterious creature,
A ghost horse
In the morning mists,
His mane gently fluttering
In the brisk breeze.
A moon stallion
In the frosty night light
His silhouette etched
Against the starry sky.
A Pegasus in my dreams
Flying free down
The milky way,
Riding the racing clouds,
With the wind
In his wings
Merging into the meadow mists
At dawn.

Victoria Stewart (9)
(Highly commended)

Spider's Prey

It was dusk,
But still
The beauty of the misty roses,
Accepted the silvery grey wonders
Of the spider web.
The spider's jealous spells whistled
Through her echoing palaces
Of silky wondrous threads.
She never regrets the passing fly
Becoming stuck.
On her spiral pavilions,
Like the flicker of a candle
The spider captures her prey,
And whilst busily weaving,
Ends her weary day.

John Gareis (13)

Of Calico Cats

Wide awake and dreaming
of calico cats,
faces white and ginger,
black and ginger,
the faces of calico cats.

You stole my glance
as I watched,
and stared at the calico cats
in the moonlight;
and under a streetlamp
I saw you standing,
standing with the calico cats.

The white is ginger,
ginger is black:
orange streetlights
cast their changeful glow.
The cats-eyes in the road
are gleaming,
and I am dreaming,
and cats are screaming,
the screams of calico cats.

Kirsty Seymour-Ure (17)
(Highly commended)

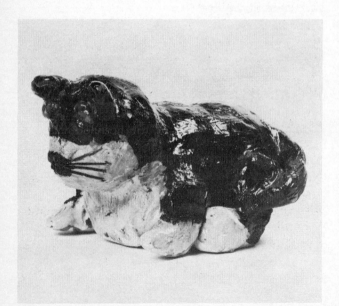

'Sparky the Cat', Graham Macmillan (7)
(Highly commended)

The Robin

A small red devil gliding elegantly,
An upturned poppy blowing in the wind.
Its graceful voice twitters in the sky.
Its long brown tail like a twig,
Trailing out of a big, rosy-red apple.
Its tiny stub of a beak pecking for worms.
Then off it goes home, gliding in the sunset.

Charlotte Haynes (10)

A Trapped Bird

A small face of scintillating black,
With beady, glittering eyes,
How depressed he looks
With fright fixed on his face.
His heart continuously beats,
His feathers contract to his body,
As he flaps and bats,
Smacking against the hard pane,
Not knowing which way to turn from the unknown
    world to freedom.
Almost unconscious, his body beating hard against a
    hand.
But soon the hand will offer freedom.

Julie Baker (11)

Oh Delicate Spider

Creeping and crawling
His legs long and thin,
Stomach, bulging like a balloon,
Waving his long legs, elegantly, in the air,
His antennae twitch as he feels his way,
Frail, but intelligent looking.
Scuttling silently across the ground,
It makes you feel amazed just to watch him
Spinning his silvery web, quickly and cleverly,
Catching flies and wrapping them in silky thread,
When outside his brown body is well camouflaged,
Curling up into a tight ball when afraid,
Moving as daintily as a ballerina,
Eyes hungry for food.

Rosalind Thirlwell (10)

The Flying Fish

Riding through the ocean waves
Silently and swiftly,
Unseen fishes gliding past
As I whirl and swirl.

Faster, faster, faster,
As I fly past coral caves,
Swordfishes and sharks cannot beat me in my race.

Away! Away! to the depths,
To the depths of the deep, deep ocean night,
Where clusters of shells and anemones wait,
Asleep on the under-sea floor.

144

Dipping, flittering and skimming through the waves
As I make my final leap into the air,
Before I drift into a tidal rocking coral-coloured
Reef.

Emily Pivonka (7)
(Highly commended)

Frog

It sits, a moist ball of flesh in my hand
Vulnerable, pressed belly close to my pink palm,
The ball of putty croaks
Blowing out with care, his throat balloon taut.
He lets it go shrivelling back into limp folds
Like worn material.
He hangs his skin cravat under his chin and smiles.
Suddenly his head jerks up
Sending black warts colliding down his back.
His eyes swivel
Full of wet black wonder
Exaggerated by the thin circlet of gold he wears
    around them.
Regally he stands
In wait for the worm, long pale pink innocence.
Then tongue whips the air and satisfaction slips down
His throat.
He presses his eyes down and shuffles his
    membraneous feet
He smiles and rests his head flacidly on my thumb.

Lisa Robinson (13)
(Award winner)

Exploration by a Foal

Lying on the grass, asleep, I feel
A warm nose pressed against my hair.
Moist breath flows into my ear. I hear
A snort, a surprised snort of a foal
Exploring the human body,
And finding, to her surprise, a nose.
Moist lips wrap around my nose, and teethless
Gums commence their sucking.
I feel a question mark rising from her head
'Where's the milk, I'm thirsty?'
Unable to breathe I shake my head and,
Like an arrow shot into a target,
The foal runs to her mother,
'Mum, mum, there's a thing over there which
    moved!'
Again I lie down and the inquisitive beast,
Slightly more warily this time,
Starts her timid exploration.
Working from my feet, she chews incessantly,
Clothes and flesh, clothes and flesh,
Up to my face.
I open my eyes to see
A tunnel lined with pink skin and whiskers,
Mud and moisture.
Her lip draws back revealing a tiny
White tooth forcing its way into the outside world.
This time she pulls my hair,
Chewing it like her mother chews the grass.
I move again, and the foal returns
To tell her mother of her discoveries.

Lucy Dixon-Clarke (16)
(Highly commended)

The Greenfinch

The greenfinch lies dead,
Never to see the blue sky,
Never to see the lush green grass.
You are still colourful, my friend.
There is no music in the air,
Your eyes are lifeless.
No more are they alert,
No more are they there to find the
      seeds I put out each day.
Little bird, there is a precious calmness
      about you
No more shall I see you.

Sadie Hill (10)

The Panda

I am a panda,
Who lives at the zoo.
My occupation is . . .
Being seen by you.
I eat eucalyptus,
For my diet,
If I don't get it
I cause a riot.

Andrea Hoy (10)

The Hunt of Rufus Red

The hunt is on! The horn resounds
And eagerly strain the baying hounds
And catch a scent across the downs
The scent of Rufus Red

The thud of hooves across the moors
Of hunters, glad to be outdoors
And 'Tally-Ho!' each rider roars
Pursuing Rufus Red

A streak of lightning, rusty red
The blood a-pounding in his head,
His mind aflame with haste and dread
The form of Rufus Red.

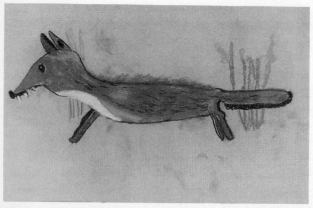

'The Fox', Joanne Morris (6)

No time to waste, no backward glance
A second, lost, would lose his chance
His eyes in wild unseeing trance
The eyes of Rufus Red

The hounds, pursuing, now come close
His tail before the leader's nose
He strains his tired, aching toes
Run faster, Rufus Red!

But weary footed, stumbling now
With strength all spent and tail hung low
The hounds lurch with triumphant row
And Rufus Red is . . . dead.

Ingrid Murray (12)
(Highly commended)

Spider

A silky web is the spider's home.
And o'er this web he's free to roam.

But let a fly try these same tricks,
And to the web he surely sticks.

The hungry spider grabs the fly,
And then injects to make him die.
Wraps him up in a silver ball
And takes him to his dining-hall.

Thomas Gallagher (12)

The Cat

The black cat from next door,
Is a fearsome creature.
With piercing green eyes, it hunts,
It kills.
The two eyes are search-lights,
Gleaming in the darkness,
Waiting to pounce on bird.
Helpless is its prey,
And I am sorrowful, when
I see flesh lying where the
Beast has left it.
Now it is I that is waiting to
Hunt, to kill even.
A smooth stone is clenched in my
Hand, and the creature is
Approaching.
I am poised, ready to fling
The stone, but I drop it seeing
Its eyes.
'Who is it sins now?'
Those eyes say.
'You the hunter, or I the prey?'

Lesley Piper (11)

The Pigeon

A bough is weeping in the stream
Green island green and, I dream,
A pigeon's moan disquiets me.

150

'Pigeons', Sin-Ti-Towlson (15)

Her breast is lapis lazuli,
Her throat is pale pistachio green,
Hazel the wing she turns to preen,
Her throbbing throat disquiets me.

Over the ruby of her eyes,
She flickers lids of pearl,
With edges of gold, when she cries,
Her note disquiets me.

She sits on the branch as if a throne,
Hiding her throat within a fold
Of her bright wing, and still her moan
Is in the air; she disquiets me.

But when my tears are my reply
Above the branch she spreads her wings
Bearing my heart away, to fly
Above despair and mortal things.
Where I can never go, ah where?
O weeping bough, I do not know.

Stephen Millar (14)
(Highly commended)

151

Tashy the School's Rabbit

We clean his play pen
    every day
When we've finished we
    go out to play.
Miss Grundy gives him her
    home-made bread,
Tashy's pram is shining
    red.
Tashy sleeps in his wooden
    hutch
We all love him very
    much.
Tashy's eyes are very bright,
His furry coat is black
    and white.
He goes home with all
    his kind friends,
We wouldn't leave
    him in school at weekends.
Sometimes he's in a
    naughty mood,
But this doesn't put him
    off his food.
Tashy runs and scampers
    free,
When he's tired he sleeps
    on my knee.
If it is warm he goes out
    on the grass,
The children shout, 'Hello'
    as they pass

Carrots, oats and pears he
    loves to eat
He then runs round Miss
    Grundy's feet.
He begs, he searches, he
    jumps on our knees
Just 'cos he's looking
    for dandelion leaves.
At home-time it's into
    his pen and close the door
Tashy settles down and
    sleeps on his straw.

Rachel Teggert (7)

The Peregrine Falcon

The falcon soars down through
    the sky like a bullet from a gun.
His eyes like the moon, his beak
    and claws like iron.
He spots a seagull below
With one swipe the seagull falls
    in a cloud of feathers.
The falcon lands gracefully
    beside it.
The dark shadow sitting handsomely
    in a darkened tree, gorged.

Gary Rous (10)

The Eccentric Elephant

There was an elephant at the zoo,
Who,
Said he was born in Timbuctoo.

There was an elephant at the zoo,
Who,
Stuck his tail on with superglue.

There was an elephant at the zoo,
Who,
Solved the problem of two times two.

There was an elephant at the zoo,
Who,
Liked his cage bars painted bright blue.

There was an elephant at the zoo,
Who,
On his foreleg had a tattoo.

There was an elephant at the zoo,
Who,
Each day for dinner ate beef stew.

There was an elephant at the zoo,
Who,
Mastered the way to use the loo.

There was an elephant at the zoo,
Who,
From the spectators caught the flu.

'Elephant'. Stephanie Keeley (16)

There was an elephant at the zoo,
Who,
Only lived until he was two.

This was an elephant at the zoo,
Who,
I wish I had met, don't you?

Helen Boddy (12)

Pigs

Pigs are big and pink and round,
They sniff along the muddy ground,
And when they see a nice soft spot,
They jump in with a happy plop.

Katie Sandford (9)

Sea Birds

The gulls hover above me,
With outstretched wing,
Swoop like a kite,
When you let go the string.

An oyster-catcher stalks
Through the wet sand,
Takes off and circles,
Then returns to the land.

A guillemot dives,
And comes up with a fish,
Swallows it whole, and
Takes off with a swish.

A cormorant jumps,
From high on its nest,
Then flies at the last moment,
And returns for a rest.

Sunlight is fading,
Birds return to their nests,
After the day's excitement,
They need a rest.

Rory James Clarke (10)

Mowgli

Nose
Wet with goodness,
Fresh and new.

His belly
Swaying from side
To side.

The tail
Long, flexible
Swiping the air

His claws
Retracting
With slow movement.

Stretching
His forelegs out in front
His back ones hidden under
His back side.

Walking
His muscles moving
Lazily under his skin.

Stuart Brazier (12)

During the nineteenth century, canaries were used by coalminers to warn them of any unknown pockets of gas. If a bird loose in a mine choked and died the miners would steer clear of that area.

Canary in a Coalmine

Blood runs,
Flags fly,
Gunshots sound;
A soldier dies.
A canary in a coalmine,
A number in a book,
A name on a war plaque
A piece of history.

How willingly did England send her young men off to
    war;
To die for a funeral of honour and flowers.
And when the lives are taken of the fearless and the
    brave,
The only remembrance is the writing on the graves.
Uniformed leaders gather more arms,
While peacemakers protest, arms entwined,
What will it take to save the world from evil-minded
    men
Who can destroy and burn the earth before you
    count to ten.
'It's not looking good,' the newspapers say,
'You can close your eyes,
But, it won't go away.
Live for today, smile, have fun,
For tomorrow may never come.'

Julie Sheriff (14)

The Arts

Dance

The laughing lightbulbs crawl
Across the throbbing wall.
Don't dance.
The kaleidoscope of light,
Screaming through the night.
Don't dance.
The sweating, crushing throng
Dances all night long,
And still the silent voice says
'Don't dance'.

Tim Footman (15)

'Tribal Mask'.
Matthew William
Barham (10)

The Piano Player

Inside the smoke
a man plays the piano
slowly, a tune he has heard
a long time ago
a friend, no, a stranger
played it to him in a pub
like this one,
now he plays it to these people,
fatandugly boring beerdrinkers,
it will change their lives, he knows
it will change their minds.

He plays, but no one listens
they drift away from the piano
towards the dartboard,
his long fingers hesitate, stammer to a
stop; the smoke curls itself lovingly
around him, and his eyes go to the bar,
his feet follow
as they have done every evening
and will do,
until his fingers stammer to a halt completely.

Emma Payne (15)

The Young Performer

Those black flowers, spattered
Across maimed, white paper
Created her dream of
A fresh, innocent spring,
Of clear water hopping
Over algae-glazed rocks.

But was it Mozart's dream?
The gifted boy who loved
Playing arpeggios
Even staccato scales.
Maybe he longed for
A new pair of shoes.

She wondered if applause
Were voluntarily
Awarded or was it
Fashionable to have
Responsive receptions,
Or sore, red, swollen hands?

Then, chuckling to herself,
She imagined critics
Slouching in the front seats,
Scribbling with blunt pencils.
Solitary, she listened
To detached orchestra.

Caressing the furled scroll,
Silently returning
Bow poised, quivering hand.
Only two bars before . . .
She lowered her hot feet,
Back in the cool water.

Jessica Owens (13)

The Dancer

Music flows.
He dances gracefully,
As light as a flame,
A motion in his fantasy,
Silent poetry,
The art of all arts,
Dancing is to live,
Emotions in the air,
Leaping,
Rotational movements.
He accelerates,
The melody quickens its pace,
Twisting,
Turning,
He moves freely,
Where his legs take him,
The dance reaches its climax,
Gradually swiftness hesitates,
Deceleration,
Still as graceful,
The music stops,
Sweat on his supple spine,
Position poised.

Rosemary Billington (14)

Art

Art is messy,
Paint everywhere.
Paint on the tables,
Paint on the chairs.
Paint on the desk lids,
Paint on the door.
Paint on the ceiling,
Paint on the floor.
Everyone likes Art,
What a merry caper;
There's paint all around the room,
But none on the paper!

Olivia Frances Hum (9)

Photographs

The nice thing about Christmas,
Is that Grandad comes to stay.
He always brings his camera,
And burns his flash away.
We have lovely pictures of ceilings,
And lovely pictures of floors.
There's lovely pictures of curtains,
And lovely pictures of doors.
There's hardly any with us on,
And those there are quite blurred.
Still, Grandad really means well,
It's only mishaps that occurred.

Janey Mitson (9)

The Race

In the dark cold frosty dawn
Bright torches shine
On the sparkling ice.
Bare black trees
By the side of windswept lakes.
Crowds thrilled, numbed by the cold,
Come to watch
The Eleven Towns Race.
Off they go!
Black shadows in a hurry
Rushing across the canal.

'Marathon '83'.
Alistair Provan (11)
(Highly commended)

The icy blasts of wind
Howl as they pass
Through the cheering crowd,
Stamping their feet,
Blowing their frostbitten fingers
To keep warm.
Not so the skaters
Kept warm by their elation,
Skating as fast as they can,
To win the race.
Puffs of white clouds,
Breathe from their dry mouths
Freezing as it comes
To the end of the punishing race.

Claire Morris (10)

The Flute-player's Flute

A stick of bamboo, a hollow stick,
A flute, sweet music.
Fingers moving over different holes.
Strange, soothing, mysterious.
Makes you feel
As if drifting up, up, up.
Happy sounds of the fresh green meadows.
The pure, narrow, running streams,
The clean air of the mountains.
Music, that beautiful music.
The music becoming faster
Then slowing down, lulling people to sleep.
Children clapping in time to the music
A flute bringing happiness and joy
In its mysterious way.

Christopher McKeag (10)

My Clown

I have a clown, his face is bright red,
He eats all my dinner and jumps on my bed,
He adores entertaining, and loves doing shows
And he makes such a racket with the trumpet he
    blows.
He throws custard pies in everyone's face
It's true that he is really a shocking disgrace,
He hides in his bed when the doorbell goes beep
And because it's not night-time he can't get to sleep.

Helen Freake (7)

Die Laughing

When the curtain falls
All is quiet,
Save the audience of mourners
Who await the fiery-hooped finale
From the sixpenny stalls.
But for them the performance is over.
Only the magicians in the carbon grey costumes
Are allowed to follow.
And while leaving some turn
To view their loss,
Washed up through the worn-out tapes of the
    baritoned choir.
Outside the dull mugworts tower the indifferent
    displays
Of dyed lilac tulips and cast-iron harps,
And far, far away lies the one who counts
Mislaid by trapdoors and 'extra' effects
To an unreachable place.

Lucy Elvidge (17)
(Highly commended)

The Singer (Standing Stone)

The world passes you by,
Sit, as you sing, smiling,
A life in each red gold tangled hair,
The cobbles hard beneath you.

Sit, as you sing, smiling,
Your guitar apricot
In the scudding sun,
In your blue green eyes holding
All the tears ever wrung.

Sit, as you sing, smiling,
And the people pass you by,
Your voice holds in a million years,
Your heart, a million skies.

Sit, as you sing, smiling,
Forever I see you there.
The church may crumble,
But on the hill,
The man with the songs fills the air.

Sarah Childs (17)
(Highly commended)

Vincent Van Gogh: The Last Self Portrait
Painted at Auvers, May 1890

In front of the mirror the ego swells:
A mutilated genius is unfurled,
A soured reaction to his private Hell,
Portrayed by a background of thrashing whirls.
The searing eyes which pierce from out of paint
Reveal the inner madness of the man.
They chant the anthem of the Anti-Saint
More potently than any landscape can.
The brooding scowl; the pointed brow
Describe the sharpness of his pain.
The stare at infinity illustrates how
To grind out meaning from a disabled brain.
    In a festival of green and blue
    Intense expression spears you.

Cheeks inscribed by fork-like brush-strokes
(Violence and beauty take turns to appear).
Hair cropped back in aquiline spokes
(A friendship severed, then an ear).
His puritanic instincts bore the South,
Affairs with asylums in Glitterland
Force panic and confusion through his mouth,
Yet all is clarified by brush in hand.
Today he can paint a masterpiece,
Tomorrow slash a lobe off with a knife;
Today he gives emotion full release,
Tomorrow he will suffocate his life.
    No drug on Earth can interrupt
    A man's desire to self-destruct.

David Woodhouse (14)
(Award winner)

To Paint a Window

First,
Paint the coldness of a window frame,
Straight,
Dripping,
Dripping with condensation.
Spill the water
On the air,
Creating the dirty glass.
Piece together the
Brush bristles
To create the misty appearance
Of frost bitten insect wings,
Then,
With a brush,
Chisel out the paint, so it flakes
On the window frame.
And then,
With a brush,
Dig,
Dig a canal for the descending
Water to escape from the window sill.
And lastly,
Mix,
Mix the ugliest green,
For the lurking putty
In the corners of the window.

And then,
It's hung on the wall.
Like a picture,
It reveals the outside world.

Karl Andrews (13)

Reflections

A Winter Remembrance

Early one winter's day I went out walking
And left my bootprints patterned in the snow.
It could have been a century ago –
No sounds of dogs or cars or people talking,
Only the wind keening as it began to blow.

I strode across the park towards the High Street.
The trees were hung with canopies of frost
And as I left the park, and as I crossed
The road, I saw that every path and by-street
Under a creaseless layer of snow was lost.

I neared the war memorial. A wreath
Still lay below it with its poppies red
And, coming closer, I saw the flowers had bled
Their dye into the icy snow beneath,
Making them blanched and cold as stone, and dead.

Arnold Hunt (14)
(Highly commended)

Parents

At the table we meet.
I am somewhere between the two.
Where, what dreams do I fulfil,
How much of an extension?
I, the silent spectator,
Watching the sorrow on their chiselled features,
Watching each guise, lovers, parents, providers . . .
In proportion to age.
Have I replaced their bed
Their duty done, product centred?
The roles for me emerge
Darker and darker by every day.
Will I be ambushed before I'm thirty,
As I have ambushed them?

Iain McKenzie (16)

'Football Crowd', group work, Oakham School, Oakham, Rutland (11)

171

Burnt at the Stake

I wince, the coarse rope cuts into my wrists,
And shuffle, seeking a more comfortable stance
On the branches, straw, dung and putrid rags.

My cheeks turn red as each eye and finger is directed
    to me,
Heartily thankful for a free afternoon's
    entertainment,
Never sparing a thought as to why I am here.

You would demand justice and support
As I do, now a friendless, sinful melancholy ruffian,
Disgraced by a few kind deeds, a free puppet show.

The tongues of fire lap the mossed, furry branches
And glow delighted at every dry twig and slim straw,
My knees weaken and fists clench, I hug the stake.

Tense as a dry twig, I squeeze my bulging eyes shut
And tears momentarily relieve my cheeks of the
    merciless, resolute heat.
Skin streams and the tongues lap my already brittle
    limbs.

Screaming like a hysterical cat when the first tongues
    lap up my feet,
I am immersed, drowned in pain, numb with fear and
    then . . .
Acceptance and careless peace and I am drawn to
    timeless rest.

Jessica Owens (13)

Shadows

Your shadow is a little spy.
He follows you around,
And when you're walking in the park
He stalks across the ground.
He imitates your every move
And never loses track,
When you suspect and turn around
He hides behind your back.
So on a hot and sunny day
Be cautious and watch out,
Your shadow will be very near
To follow you about.
This funny black mischievous man,
You never see his face,
But when the sun's behind a cloud
He's vanished into space.

Michael Castleton (10)

The Conflict

There was silence –
Silence as the clouds crossed the sky
An overpowering sense
Of the day that would not die,
As a curtain on the glitt'ring stage
The dark grey o'er the blue,
With one last burst of courage
In the west the inferno grew.
Then suddenly upon the scene
The silver Diana came;
All around her a misty gleam –
The searchlight of her fame.

So face to face the opponents stood,
The great powers of the sky,
But Fate had predetermined who
Would always, always die.
With a silver star as a dagger
Clenched menacing in her hand,
Diana made Hyperion stagger
And answered Fate's command.
Some day Hyperion may conquer
But until that time, on high
In the nocturnal throne sits Diana,
And the blood of the Sun tints the sky.

Clare Griffiths (13)

Fear

Man
weir
splash
fear
. . . silent
alive?
Dead.
On a soft permanent bed.

Camilla Ford (12)

Not a Child Any More

When the things you have accepted all your life,
As fact,
Become illogical;
When love first hits you,
Knocking you over with its strength;

When natural, childish selfishness leaves,
Taking innocence with it;
When the realization of the screaming, dying world,
Full of unwanted, unloved people
Plants its image before your eyes;
Then childhood goes,
Running from you,
Leaving you empty, unconfident, afraid.
You're not a child any more.

Octavia Nicholson (14)

Thoughts of the War

Men's silhouettes on the battlefield,
Mothers explaining, 'Daddy's gone,'
To drowning memories lovers yield,
Sounds in our hearts a disillusioned song.

Poisoned minds become the fashion,
Blood-stained poppies, the season's flower,
Heartbreak, betrayal, followed by cold passion,
Behind the innocent murderers cower.

Smoke drifting in a blackening sky,
Empty shells masquerading as men,
Is this the end coming nigh?
The devil calling us to his den?

Lisa Moody (14)

Life

Life is like a fancy dress costume.
I wonder, Who wore it before us?

Charlotte Little (14)

Truth is an Onion

Lies,
the brown-yellow brittle skin
of an onion.
Truth,
the pure, white heart.

To find the truth
you must peel away,
and look beyond
the thin, brittle layers
of lies.

Man may not like the truth.
It may make man cry.
So man uses lies
to cover it up,
to keep it from being found.

Loukas Bizios (13)

Remembrance

Scrambling through the undergrowth,
Gasping for breath, heart pumping wildly,
Pushing the tall creepers to one side.
A burst of gunfire to the left,
Thudding of a body falling to the ground,
Movement in front, running away.
Sweat pouring down a hot face,
The grinding of teeth and a rip of cloth,
A movement to the right.
Over there!
Muscles bulging, tense;
Lifting a rifle
A shot echoing through the silence,
A piercing scream
The Enemy falls dead,
Blood trickling from his brow
Mixing with perspiration . . .

The old one-legged man
Sat on the park bench
Watching the small boys with sticks
Running down the path.
'Bang! Bang! you're dead!'
A make-believe scream,
The Enemy fell down,
And as he watched, he remembered.

Alistair McLeish (12)

Fear

The little short cut home,
Seemed twice as long that night.
The sky was far too dark,
The stars were not as bright.
Every leaf that fell,
All the sounds she heard,
Every little movement,
Made her feel more scared.
But still she carried on,
Along that moonlit path,
The eeriness got to her,
She thought she heard a laugh.
At last she saw a light,
Far away that's true,
Just a few feet further,
Her street would be in view.
She heard a sound behind her,
And swiftly turned to find
A man coming towards her,
With a knife glinting in his hand.
The evil fellow chuckled,
And the girl shook with fear.
He moved his face near to hers,
His breath was full of beer.
Quickly she kicked him,
And escaped while he was down,
Tripping over rocks and stones.
Trying to get into her town.
At last she reached her house,
Once inside she locked the door.
A man's cough came from the kitchen.
The killer was back for more.

Joanna Cole (14)

Barriers

Standing behind the sheet of glass
He presses his nose to its icy surface,
Watching their laughter,
Their happiness is his destruction,
His defeat.

The pane reflects his image,
Oddly constructed, 'matchstick',
Martian clothes, too smart,
Bulging in incorrect proportions,
His downfall.

Trapped in a world of hostility,
Questions stabbing his actions,
Hurt and neglect surround his shell
Of unwanted friendship,
His fate.

Hate surges forth,
His heart echoes with loneliness,
He hurls himself at the barrier,
It vibrates. There is no shatter, no escape,
His destiny.

There is no sympathy,
No welcoming arms for an outsider,
Recognized by his faults.
And who is to blame? 'Surely not us,
He is the outsider, *he* must be to blame.'

And so he is left,
In a deserted playground.

Amanda Lunt (14)

My Imagination

My imagination is like a yo-yo
Bounding up and down,
Whirling round on a string,
Reaching out for ideas,
Bright colours and patterns
Dancing around for joy.
Sometimes it gets in a tangle,
Whirls slowly
And then stops.

Joanna Childs (11)

Silence

Silence is a cool breeze lovely in your face.
   Silence is the night creeping over field and hill.
Silence is the moving tree which the wind may blow.
   Silence is the creeping mouse after all the cheese.
Silence is the moving clouds gentle over the moon.
   Silence is the snowflake dropping gently to the
      ground.

Andrew David Wright (9)

Memories

Now I am old
As fragile as the snowflakes.
Now I am slow
As slow as the summer coming.

No more can I hear
The carol singers singing.
No more can I hear
The laughter of children.

Once I could run, skip and jump
Now movement is pain.

Natasha Byrne (10)

'The Grandmother', Amanda Giffitty (15)

Am I real?

Am I real?
Or am I a dream?
Am I someone else's dream and
When they are asleep, is it daytime for me
And when they wake up from the dream
Is it night-time for me?
And when they die
Do I die?
Or am I real?
I don't know
I think I'm real – but am I?
You never know.
You can be walking to school,
Get knocked down
And die
But find yourself at school,
And after school you walk home,
Enter the house
And find yourself in a strange building.
Well – is that a fact?
Do we exist?
We don't know
You could be pictures
Illustrating a story that
Someone else is dreaming.
We don't know do we?

Lillian Kerry (11)

Making a Dream

The old greenhouse at the end of our street,
Is where the dreams are made for the town.
Yes! The small little street
Where PC Jones does his beat.
The greenhouse may look old
But even so you will be told
It's the place where the dreams are made.

Inside there is a TV screen
And a very old man who is tall and lean.
They call him the chief dream-keeper
And he lets out a dream with a button
Which sounds like a bleeper.

But inside it is more complicated by far
Because there are colourful ideas
Which are kept in a big jam-jar.
Then the little men come out
And race around and whizz about;
They are the cooks who cook the dream
And all you can smell is a dreamy smell
In the smokes and steams.
They cook the dreams for about an hour
Then they keep the ones which are sweet and throw
    away the sour.

Then a little person
With a tape measure round his neck
Makes sure the dreams are thoroughly checked.

He measures them for size
And wraps them up in newspaper which he ties.
He never makes mistakes,
For he is very wise.

Next the dreams go in a tunnel long and narrow
Where they are picked up by a sparrow
Who takes them to an office where they sort them
    into piles,
And then they send them off over many miles
To the people by whom the dreams are used
And dreams tell them tales, stories and news.

That is the end of a dream
Who now has lost his sparkle and gleam
And is burnt on a rubbish heap,
Who fades away and falls asleep.

Clare Briscoe (10)

Where am I?

I am the confusion in your head.
I am your blood rushing through you.
I am the good and bad of you.
I am your pulse pounding in you.
I am the heart pumping blood to your body.
I am your view from your eyes.
I am the brain telling you the answer to this poem.
I am the rain refreshing the ground.
I am the sun drying the washing.
I am the woodlice eating the plants.
I am the rabbit flattening the ground.
I am the dew keeping the ground moist.
I am the picture on the bare wall.
I am the cat purring in the night.
I am the mouse squeaking at dusk.
I am the wind whistling through crevices.
I am the water gushing through pipes.
I am the straw waiting to be sucked.

Daniel Matjasz (10)

Poem of Protest

Poem of Protest, he told us to write.

Poem of Protest indeed.

Why I could protest on lots of things
Like going to bed,
Or nettle stings,

But I think I'll protest on writing a
Poem of Protest, that protests about things.

Katie Joanne Burrows (11)

Old Age

Rough, wrinkled, scarred, cold skin.
Fingers like matches,
Bony, thin.
Limps on one leg.
Tries to move about.
Nothing to do.
No place to go.
Wait for a visitor,
And wait,
Wait,
Wait.

Jason Crump (11)

Experience

I am the bewilderment
That enters unfamiliar surroundings.
I am the person
Who operates the puppets' strings.
I am the alert eyes
That study every move.
I am the confidence
Of every passing thought.
I am the numbness
Of a frosty wilderness.

You are the future
Of unsuspecting thrills.
You are the battle
Of continual war.
You are the confusion
Of the everlasting world.
You are the decision,
Of every passing year.

Jenny Elizabeth Reindorp (10)

The Silent Destiny

The sun has almost gone
Behind the ancient oak; it half shows itself.
The tree is a lonely silhouette
   On the nearly bare hillside.
See its mouldering branches –
How they look like old, gnarled fingers
   On a hand
   That has known hard work in younger days.
Discarded nests
   Make the hands look knobbly and frail,
Ready to die with the sun.
As the sun disappears, the tree's destiny is certain,
Battered by the angry breath
   Of the inescapable gale.
Hardly a sound is heard
   As the soft, mouldy old trunk
   Collapses.
The moon appears,
Gazing upon the disintegrating oak,
   She weeps for the only reminder –
Tiny, brittle fragments
   Of the song-thrush's eggs.

Nicola Jane Field (10)

L'esprit

Pacing the familiar, well-worn thought circles,
Dogmas and concepts crunch underfoot.
Transcending the senses, consciousness beckons,
Deep in the darkest recesses of thought.

A whirlpool of emotions, noisily floodlit,
Recedes into distance as the tide ebbs away.
The neuron-paths wander uncertainly on,
And thousands of millions of eyes turn away.

The fog on the moor hides the circles of stone,
Like teeth biting words of contempt.
The grass and the ghosts, in pale windswept forms,
And the sound of the wind, go unheard.

The room's walls are rounded, buried in memory,
Dimly lit by one or two candles
The mind's eye looks elsewhere, leaving deep-locked
A helix-bound dark chest of treasure.

Heaven and Hell and Reality mingle
Like pools of forgotten, dark water
In the central grey chasm of consciousness –
Far above is the concept of God.

On the plateau, surrounded by vivid stars,
Many-coloured and magical light,
Meaning and logic, moral justice and truth,
And the only true horizon infinity.

Contrasting megaliths, garishly decorated
With an ambiguous portrait of the mind –
The smash of the music of triumph fades out
And the silence returns with real life.

Jonathan Harley (15)
(Highly commended)

'Pressure (City on my Back)', Carol Day (17)

Hot to Clockwork

Voluntary slaves of time
We rise from timeless dreams,
From nocturnal emotions
Just as strong as their daylight brothers,
My abstract thoughts whisk me
From situation to situation
And I am a slave of fear, hate,
Happiness and yearning love,
My brain a time machine.

I have power over time
And can experience mature delights
That daylight denies me.
My brain, senses and body recoil
As I am rudely pushed out of the door
Of my subconscious mind,
Like a drunken man from a night-club.
I rise half-conscious from my sleep
And automatically strap time like handcuffs to my
    wrist,
A voluntary slave of time.

Alison Frost (16)

Lessons

I saw you in the street today.
You at your bus-stop,
Me at mine.
Facing each other.
Separated by a small stretch of tarmac.
Or was it more than that?
Memories of the childish pranks
Encouraged by your bets and dares.
We led you on,
Yet you led us.
I never knew which
For sure.
Our eyes meet at last
Amidst the crowd.
I wait for recognition.
I saw you in the street today.
You did not know me.

Lorraine Grant (17)

Life and Death

The Thief of my Attention

That bundle of love that is coming;
Suddenly a telephone call,
A girl, yes or no?
Yes, the room sings with joy.

I sit in the corner, bewildered,
She is the thief of my attention.
I am confused,
In the play of life I am no longer a star,
I am now an understudy.

They crowd around the cot,
A gurgle and hysterical laughter erupts from the
    room.
I sit, ignored, in a corner,
No longer am I a star.

That pink ball of love
Steals my limelight.
'Get the nappies,' someone shrieks.
Why do I have to rush to and fro?

I sit down despising that pink bundle of love.
Why? Why me?
I attention-seek to no avail.
Will anything work?

Does anybody notice
When I show my latest trick?
Or does anyone laugh
When I make a joke?

Every day they question me
'How's the baby then?'
On and on.
Why do they not notice me?

Have I faded away?

James Davey (11)

Tomorrow

Death-dark cries haunt the air,
A spectre of grey people
Intoxicated in gloom.

Carefully the baby is wrapped;
A bundle of skin the epitaph
To a life deep in poverty.

Quietly, the mother weeps.

Tonight the coal fire
Burns contentedly.
It mirrors our glow of warmth.

The TV set spews a monologue
Of death and desperation.
Nonchalantly, we flick a switch

And gaze smugly.
Everyone is guilty
But we are not to blame.

Slowly, in another world,
The child rises, unsteadily,
Like a new-born calf.

A flock of flies descend.
They land their target
With a searing sizzle.

Weakly, the child collapses.

Tomorrow he will die.

We yawn, and go to bed.

Simon Ponsford (17)

Philistine

Fleshy façade of stone
With grey, grey eyes
Unfeeling, lined with rime.
Light that shies
A cast of shadow.
Moon-faced man of lies.
An ice cold facia upon which
Alba flakes melt and die.

Simon Coughlan (16)

To Lose a World

At the end of the day
A siren wails
The sound pricks us like needles –
We are unaware of what is going on.
Even as the announcer's voice
Begins to tremble
With the grave message
We are unsure.
High in the clouds
Sailing towards us
With pinpoint accuracy
Calling in on each one of us personally –
As if to show us the way out of the world
To leave behind the remains
Of our precious little life
That we collected in a mere few thousand years.

Douglas Bohn (14)

Half Life

In shadow through the peaceful trees
The steady air flows soft and cool
We went there once in silent ease
Trapped by shades, obscure but free
We went there once before the call
Wise and blind, not yet deceived.

First we left the trees behind
To venture out into the night
On moon-washed turf now unconfined
But too adventurous in our flight.

And then we left the dark behind
As dawn drew on forgot the night
Far greater things we had in mind
Desired the colours of the light.
Thrilling spectrums came to find
But they were bright and made us blind.

Nigel Blackman (16)

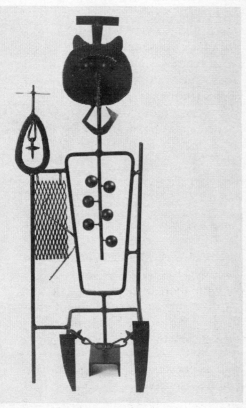

'Lady Sitting in the Park', Adrian Redmond (16)
(Highly commended)

Slow Motion

In the secret dark
Of the morning
I dreamed of you.
Dawn-lit, and favoured by flaming suns,
You wandered through my mind.

One by one the swans
Challenged the sky,
And I flew to join them.
From below you watched me,
Your face up-turned
And pleading.
So I came to rest on the lake,
In slow motion.

Kirsty Seymour-Ure (17)

Waking

Confusion of sleep-drugged dreams,
outside noises filter through,
and mingle with the thoughts
of fused experiences.
A film projection
of yesterday and tomorrow and today –
Who knows?

A mind of messed up mixed ideas
for each new
wakening moment.
As sunlight seeps into the room
so it fills my head,
clearing cobwebs from the corners
of my mind.
A bright new day, a bright new person –
ready to pre-act
tomorrow's dreams.

Rachael Jane Gregory (16)

Tomorrow

The lost and far dark memories
Of that evening's silence
Draw on my paper heart.
Those hasty words, which sounded so easy,
Are now only whispers left of promise.
In the dusk of the night,
I'm lost here by myself.

The smile of the setting sun;
A feast for the eyes,
Haunts me and leaves me glowing hopeless,
Drawing on the quiet warmth
That I once felt.
Now I don't know what to say or do.
I'm lost within myself.

The scented echoes from the past take hold,
The smell of regret,
Of the wounds of love that never heal,
Rise as tall as the blackened sky in my head,
And the night's empty air
Reflects the promise of a past evening's silence,
As I lie here by myself.

The mourning sun plays truant on my sleeping heart.
A remembrance of the night the past eclipsed the
    sun.
A hope for the day
When the echoed smell is sweet,
And the smile of the setting sun warms the coldness I
    feel.
Until then I just keep my cares deep within,
And pray for what hope tomorrow might bring.

Simon Poole (17)

Broken Time

The curious watch observes the world
Through broken face of splintered glass
Viewing, unbelievingly,
The silent seasons as they pass.
His aching hands have long since stopped
As rust, like rheumatism, came.
And now he thinks that time's gone mad
Not knowing why, or who to blame.
For plants have bloomed, have grown, have died,
And petals fallen to the ground
To slowly fade like morning mist
And disappear without a sound.
While the watch's hands don't even twitch
To register that time has passed.
And so the watch remains confused
How could a year go so fast?

He sits upon his dusty sill
And stares beyond the window pane
Longing for normality
To show the minutes move again.
But none will come to fix the watch
That does not know it's wrong;
That spends what seems eternity
Before a second's gone . . .

I was curious to open the door and see
What lay within its tortured soul
That caused him so much misery
And stop the man from being whole
But even while I pondered this
The door began to open wide
And through the flitting shadows
I could see what lay inside.

A withered man was beckoning
'Come follow!' through bad teeth he wheezed.
He gave a grin of dark decay
And my shivering arm he seized.
He dragged me down into his pit
And in the blackness I could see
A thousand faces on the walls
With eyes that stared right into me.
Each head portrayed a type of pain
And cries for help were all around
And yet the cripple dragged me on
While faces faded without sound.
Twisted ghosts leapt from the depths
Like dreams that must not really be.
Their jagged claws that ripped so deep,
Their spirits, anger, jealousy . . .
Emotions screamed within my mind
As hatred beat upon my brain
And spite just taunted, mockingly
Forever hissing out my name.
And the old man slowly turned,
Face rotting right before my eyes,
And shrieked his laughter all around
While sanity just knelt and cried . . .

Christopher Lawrence (17)

Graveyard

The clock strikes,
     once,
          twice, over and over,
               menacingly.
Gargoyles leer from jagged crevices;
     moths surround me,
          silent and grey,
     flitting through the graveyard
  like small, deadly sentinels.
In the distance,
          warmth and comfort,
  a loving smile and snug bed.
               Can I reach it?
Something silvery on silken thread
               descends.
  I cannot move;
          fear holds me here,
          grabs at my hair,
          laughs in my face,
          pulls and pinches me,
          binds and sneers at me,
               then suddenly
          pushes and jolts me.
     I cannot bear it!
               I run.
          Thorn trees,
     twisted,
  evil,
reach out their gnarled arms
     to grab me.
  The air is cold
     but the wind is still.

My flickering lantern
     dims,
   then dies.
I hate the dark!
I fear fear itself!
   My legs
  cannot give in,
and carry me forward.
   All around
     is a queer feeling
almost a premonition,
  and as I approach
   I see the truth.
  My way is blocked!
     Twisting, I turn down a dark alley,
I mustn't give up!
  I come out into a lit street,
    a familiar avenue.
Fear shrinks back to its lair
   to wait for another
     victim.

Fiona Helen Van Ryne (11)

Star Wars

Rebel fleets already formed
Out of the rebel base they swarmed
Zooming, zooming, flying high
Going far beyond the sky.
'Set course for lasers – fire at base
We've got to save the human race'
Enemy base coming into sight,
OK boys we'll stay and fight
Any good hits set chain reactions
Blow this junk-heap into fractions

Into the death-stars' tunnel we go,
If we win we'll let you know
'Red five going in.' 'Fire at will,'
'Take him down, the poor man's ill,'
'Cruising in now: switch to main'
Save us from Darth Vader's reign.

David Exton (10)

Index of titles

Index of authors

The 1985 Cadbury's Poetry Competition

The Cadbury's Books of Children's Poetry contain about 200 selected entries from children of all ages and are illustrated with work from the National Exhibition of Children's Art.

If you would like to enter the 1985 competition whether in the Art, Craft or Poetry sections, you can write to this address for an order form:

Cadbury's National Exhibition of Children's Art
Granby
Altrincham
Cheshire
WA14 5SZ
(Please enclose a stamped/addressed envelope)

Remember – you not only have a chance to feature in the *Cadbury's Third Book of Children's Poetry* but also to win a place on the Cadbury Italian Art Tour.